P9-EFG-125

DISCARDED

THE DESIGNS OF ACADEMIC LITERACY

A Multiliteracies Examination of Academic Achievement

Michael Newman

BERGIN & GARVEY
Westport, Connecticut • London

Library of Congress Cataloging-in-Publication Data

Newman, Michael, 1957 Jan. 15–
    The designs of academic literacy : a multiliteracies examination of academic
achievement / Michael Newman.
        p.   cm.
    Includes bibliographical references and index.
    ISBN 0–89789–837–0 (alk. paper)
    1. Academic achievement—Case studies.   2. College students—Case studies. 3.
Motivation in education—Case studies.   I. Title.
    LB1062.6.N49   2002
    370.15′4—dc21   2001043013

British Library Cataloguing in Publication Data is available.

Copyright © 2002 by Michael Newman

All rights reserved. No portion of this book may be
reproduced, by any process or technique, without the
express written consent of the publisher.

Library of Congress Catalog Card Number: 2001043013
ISBN: 0–89789–837–0

First published in 2002

Bergin & Garvey, 88 Post Road West, Westport, CT 06881
An imprint of Greenwood Publishing Group, Inc.
www.greenwood.com

Printed in the United States of America

The paper used in this book complies with the
Permanent Paper Standard issued by the National
Information Standards Organization (Z39.48–1984).

10   9   8   7   6   5   4   3   2   1

Contents

Figures and Tables

FIGURES

TABLES

Preface

The present study was inspired by some admittedly naive but profound questions that arose when I was in graduate school and teaching developmental courses including college reading and ESL in various colleges in City University of New York. My students had not only placed into these classes, but many also had great trouble working their way out of what was officially considered at best a *semi*-college sequence. While I was teaching them, I began to wonder what exactly separated them from their peers, sometimes of identical socioeconomic status, who were considered proficient. Precisely what was it that other students could do that mine had so much trouble with? Was it what they knew, in the sense of content? Well, many did seem to be shockingly ignorant in some matters that seem commonly assumed to be known by educated people. Some did not know the components of the solar system, while others thought that Los Angeles was a state, and a few could not spell words like "would" or "people." But the mere lack of such knowledge only begs the question of why had they not picked up those "basic" facts to begin with.

Was it that they had difficulty learning generally? A few may have had this kind of systematic problem, but most had learned a lot of things that I did not know, sometimes complex ones, even if they did not count academically. Some could tell me subtle differences between Bachata, Merengue, Salsa, and Son, together with corresponding dance steps at a high level of intricacy. Others knew the Bible backward and forward. Still others had an impressive knowledge of sports trivia, of romance novels, of fashion, or of the origins and ideologies of various youth gangs. Others could explain the evolution of graffiti writing styles from their origin in the 1970s on down. If something mattered to them, they could clearly learn it, but, although they all claimed that college was extremely important to them, they could not figure their way out of the remedial system.

Did they lack certain basic academic communication skills such as reading or logical reasoning? Well some said they had never actually read a book, and when faced with one, even of their own choosing, did not seem to know what to do with it. Yet others could find intelligent things to say about *Crime and Punishment, Caged Bird,* or intricate Tony Hillerman mysteries that taught Navajo cosmology along the way. Their arguments placed in five-paragraph format were often rudimentary and puerile, but I overheard intricate oral back and forths on the existence of God and the moral consequences of that existence or lack of it. Pretty abstract stuff.

Was it that the measures we were using were just inappropriate? Well, one taxi driver who got a C in my class—and that was a bit of a gift—managed to get a full scholarship to MIT, but he certainly was an exception. The vast majority did poorly across the curriculum—the advocates of mainstreaming notwithstanding—and often caused dismay among the regular faculty and sometimes their classmates who looked at their work. If the assessments were wrong, then they were wrong in college generally, and I could not get out of my head that the ones we were giving just were not that hard. A five-paragraph essay responding to a question no one really cares about—the test that we used to place and exit the program—is not a good measure of writing, and it has been abolished since (along with many of the programs, I should add). However, many of the nondevelopmental students could have managed a coherent, passing response in the tenth grade. The same can be said for the even more flawed reading test, which was passed at a tenth- or eleventh-grade level. The problem was more basic than the assessments. There was clearly some disconnect involving academic literacy in general. I wanted to know what that disconnect was.

My research as a doctoral student did not address these questions. It involved the systematicity of pronoun agreement in discourse. Of course, I was also learning about literacy research in some of my classes, about the role of culture, about literacy as ideological in nature, about learning as a social phenomenon, and so on. These approaches to the problem of my students were clearly far more insightful than my work on pronouns. Their truths were evident in the faces of my students, mostly first- or second-generation immigrants of Third World origin or African Americans. This research explored the "ways with words" across students' lives and the relations between academics and vernacular literacy. Similar truths could also be found in critical works that examined how academic norms maintained and justified power relations. However, neither tradition states exactly what it takes to succeed in college, the nitty-gritty mechanics of success. Some of the other types of work that I examined by contrast explored smaller issues, focusing on components of the academic system such as reading, studying, or writing. No one explored what academic literacy actually consisted of across classes and modalities, what made it "academic" literacy. This was my ultimate naive and profound question: What is academic literacy?

The answer you have in the remainder of the book is the result of eleven weeks of data gathering with four so-called proficient undergraduates, their teachers, and the literacy artifacts they produced together. It is also the result of five years of efforts to make sense of the data found during that brief period plus one year of writing. These exploratory efforts took me to literature in various disciplines, including literacy, information theory, composition, and cognitive science. It also involved a continual revisiting of the data and seeing how data informed my understanding of the literature. In the end it left me with the conclusion that academic literacy is its own activity. It is a game played by its particular rules and following its particular principles. The rest of this book is a description of that game.

Acknowledgments

My first thanks go to those I cannot name, at least by their real names. They include first of all the four students who participated in weekly sessions in my office for ten weeks, as well as the five professors, whom I saw only once. All gave of themselves in ways that went beyond the commitment to meet me. None recieved any sort of compensation beyond what they got by sharing their thoughts. Nothing that follows would be possible without them.

I would also like to thank those who have read, criticized, and commented on parts of this work written or presented or have supported it in other ways. They include Nathalie Bailey, George Newell, Rob Tierney, Ann Johns, Vladimir Sloutsky, David Hanauer, and Matt Mitchell. Naturally, they bear no responsibility for the parts that they disagree with. I have special thanks to Jerome Mescher, who as a research assistant transcribed many of the interviews and participated fully in most, adding his own insights. He helped make it not only fruitful, I at least believe, but also enjoyable.

My final thanks go to Hevert Rodriguez for his help in preparing the copies of the students' notes and exams for publication and for teaching me how to use Adobe Photoshop in the process. In addition, I am grateful to Donna Bierschwale and The Robert F. Wagner Secondary Schoool for the Arts and Technology for letting me use their equipment (and Hevert's time) in the process.

ORIENTATION

Part I of the book is designed as an orientation process that repeats my own five years of exploration of the academic literacy game. Chapter 1 introduces readers to a way of focusing on academic literacy as its own unique problem. I frame the issue as not entirely resolvable in terms of any other area of research. In other words, my argument is that academic literacy is not cognitive psychology, sociology, composition, or even genres, but it needs its own approach within literacy theory. I argue that this approach needs to be framed in terms of information, which is the material used in the game. An exploration involves explaining what the game consists of and describing the skills that make a player more or less competent.

Chapter 2 provides a three-part literature review that first surveys educational research that touches on information, second describes information theory, and then finally integrates that theory with the Multiliteracies Project, which provides a framework for analysis. The chapter closes with the traditional research questions.

Chapter 3 provides a description of the methods, which involved the qualitative multicase study approach that has become standard in socially based literacy research. It shows how research subjects were chosen and investigated, and how the data were gathered and analyzed.

Chapter 4 balances that analytic framework with a human dimension. It introduces readers to the participants as four unique people living their lives and playing the "academic achievement game" as only one part of a full human existence.

Chapter 1

Introduction

MAKING A DIFFERENCE IN PEOPLE'S LIVES

How to be successful in college is, like how to get rich, a paradigmatic example of an ill-structured problem, meaning that it cannot be formalized and so is not consistently solvable, at least by algorithmic means. The most obvious source of the ill structure is undoubtedly the vagueness of the term "success." Nevertheless, even if the imprecision were resolved by operationalizing that concept as achieving above a certain grade point average (GPA)—and I will defend this stipulation shortly—the ill structure does not disappear. There is no consistently winning prescription for getting high grades. Even broad, common-sense recommendations such as "study often" or "do your assignments diligently" can be countered with too many exceptions. There are, we must admit, plenty of students whose assiduousness is met with disappointment and others who, despite general carelessness and slacking, receive excellent grades, at least in some classes. The ill structure, then, derives not only from vagueness but also from inconsistency and mutability; it is as if students are faced with a game whose rules are constantly in flux in sometimes unpredictable ways.

Yet it is also true that certain students tend to do better than others consistently across terms, courses, and disciplines, and there are others whose success appears to be conditioned by certain factors such as subject, task type, and/or modality of expression. Finally, there are those who start out doing poorly despite considerable effort but appear to learn something that makes for sustained improvement at some point in their academic careers. Similar patterns can no doubt be found for getting rich, again dodging the issue of what "getting rich" means by stipulating an operational definition such as accumulating a certain amount of capital.

These apparent differences in ability imply that some people have more of some kinds of knowledge, or at least facility at gaining that knowledge, than others in these domains. The presumed existence of these forms of knowledge constitutes an opening for research on various factors associated with achieving success. This work includes forms of educational research in the one case, and business studies in the other. Such disciplines will never be hard science perhaps, but they are considered of value and in the case of business classes, enough so that taking business classes can be *one part* of an individual's effort to get rich. They tell us something about the processes involved.

Of course, it would be utterly misleading—if not infuriating—for me to propose that research on postsecondary education actually tries to solve the problem of "how to be successful in college." By the same token, I can almost see my business colleagues squirming at the notion that they investigate "the science of getting rich." In both cases, such impossible prescriptions are best left for authors of books designed for the gullible. Perhaps one mode of getting rich is to write these kinds of books. Instead, at least in the case of education, the exploration is of aspects of certain processes related to what students, teachers, institutions, and societies do in and for education. Examples in postsecondary education have included exploring the effects of study and learning strategies, characterizing student behaviors, examining the writing processes of individual students, and exploring social and affective factors, among many other issues. While varied, these targets of research are far more tightly delimited than "success," and they are well-defined enough for a systematicity of some kind to become visible. They are also small enough for a relatively full picture of the processes in question to emerge.

Yet in the end, education, like business, is an area of *applied* research, and as such its justification is that it makes a difference in people's lives. That "difference" should lead to greater success for more people, and whether we like it or not, students, faculty, and administrations have operationalized *one form of success* through the grading system. We may be aware of the many inadequacies of that system, and a few educational institutions have felt it to be pernicious enough to eliminate (portions of) it, but it is still one of the most pervasive features of education over time and location. If nothing else, it determines one kind of success, much the way gaining wealth determines one kind of success in the business world.

The point is that it is a legitimate and interesting problem to try to better understand how students go about achieving grades—what I call "academic achievement." It could even be argued that it is a moral imperative to do so. After all, it is a system that we academics have created and that we re-create every day we teach and assess. We usually use it not only to assess but also to influence our students' behavior. We really should understand what we are putting them through, particularly since it has tangible effects on their lives. Therefore, it is also a legitimate and interesting applied problem to understand what it is higher-achieving students know or can grasp that their less successful counterparts do not know or cannot figure out. As that knowledge is revealed, it becomes possible to pass on some of it to the lower achievers; at least it is worthwhile trying to do so.

The problems of *what* academic achievement means to students and *which processes* are associated with different levels of performance are the starting points of this qualitative multicase study. In it, I explore these issues as they relate to four undergraduate social science majors with quite different GPAs at a major U.S. public research institution I call "Midwestern State University" (MSU). I examine how these research participants went about achieving their grades, what they thought they were doing, and how they evaluated their efforts. I also look at their achievement from other angles, those of the products they produced that led directly to their grades, including exams, oral presentations, exercises, and papers. I also examine the oral and written texts they interacted with as part of their efforts and the perspectives of a number of their professors. Although I am aware that others may have other referents for this term and other names for what I am observing, I call the set of competencies that lie behind their achievement *academic literacy*.

THE LAW OF HERE

One reason for using the term *academic literacy* in this way is that the study falls methodologically and epistemologically within the tradition of the New Literacies Studies (Street 1993, 1995) or Socioliteracy (Johns 1997). Consequently, I assume an understanding of literacy as a social phenomenon rather than as purely cognitive processing, linguistic issues, or manipulating graphic forms of language. More specifically, academic literacy is assumed to constitute a practice in the sense of Lave and Wenger (1991). This practice links individual decisions, motives for these decisions, and their effects within the set of social norms that govern behavior of the members of an academic community. In the words of the case-study participant I will be calling "Will," it is "the law of here," meaning the university.

As in other socioliteracy studies, the findings are not meant to be understood as generalizations or claims about academic literacy as a general phenomenon but are asserted as facts only for the cases examined. They are suggested as possibilities elsewhere, suggestions regarding where to look in other research and hypotheses that may be confirmed as generalized patterns in other types of studies. Furthermore, the phenomena studied are naturalistic rather than induced, even in such qualitative formats as think-aloud protocols, not to mention experimental tasks or specially designed assignments. However, I should hasten to add that the work does not constitute an ethnography because I did not engage in participant observation. Instead, following the standard practice in socioliteracy studies in higher education, I collected data largely through open-ended retrospective interviews and linguistic and genre analysis of documents.

Socioliteracy has developed into a broad tradition of research, and it provides a number of ways to narrow down the ill-structured issue of academic success to a size that can be usefully attacked. In this study, I focus on the framework of semipredictable norms of communication (Bartsch 1987) in which students and teachers operate. This assumption places this study within one of the most recent and exciting developments in literacy research, the Multiliteracies Project (New London Group 1996/2000; Cope and Kalantzis 2000b). Multiliteracies allows me to explain this kind of normative system as a "Design," roughly the structuring of a literate system (Kress 2000). The ambiguity between nominal and verbal dimensions of the gerund *structuring* is deliberate. The Design, in its noun sense, serves as a set of available resources for communication for literates, the way that grammar does for speakers of a language. The idea is that to be literate in a particular domain means to know the overlapping and interactive set of organizational resources shared by participants that enables communication to take place in that domain. In particular, Design provides the predictability needed to communicate.

In its verb sense, to Design is to produce a structure. The idea is that literate individuals Design their communicative efforts as they go along, and therefore to communicate is to create structure socially. Again grammar provides a good illustration. The structure of the grammar is not only knowledge, but it also emerges in the utterance spoken, which is why we can diagram a sentence. More important, the inherence of the structure in the utterance is essential for language to be acquired since it can be inducted by the language learner.[1] The emergent aspect to Design, the act of Designing, also creates flexibility; it is possible for Designs to change as communication takes place since individuals can and do alter some of the rules they are following as they go along. Wittgenstein (1953) referred to this phenomenon in his discussion of how people change the rules of what he called "language games" as they "play." Because the game is in some sense defined by its rules, changing the rules slightly changes the game. Since individual literates can shift the rules at will or by error, their interlocutors may be faced with variations in Design and therefore somewhat varied games. The price of flexibility and transmissibility is ill structure. Knowledge of a Design, then, is knowledge of a mutable and so inevitably somewhat ill-structured system.[2]

Also in accordance with the Multiliteracies framework, the academic literacy I explore is multimodal, including not only written language but also oral language, graphics, bubble sheets, and mathematical or chemical formulas. None of the modalities is a priori preeminent because the ultimate issue in literacy is Design, which can be found in any modality or by combining them. Gee (1989, p. 9)—one of the New London Group (NLG) members—argues that the insistence on maintaining "print" in a definition of literacy implies an acceptance of "reading and writing as a set of decontextualized isolable skills." It also obeys a time, quickly passing, in which print had an exalted role in western culture (Gee 2000), what I have elsewhere called "the cult of the written word" (Newman, forthcoming).

Finally, Design is a social construct in the sense that it is the product of the functional needs of its users/producers. Previous work in socioliteracy has emphasized the role of culture in determining characteristics of academic literacy. For example, Scollon (1995), Pennycook (1996), and Ramanathan and Atkinson (1999) have all discussed the roots of such literacy practices as plagiarism in the individualistic value systems of Western society. However, NLG members Cope and Kalantzis (2000a, pp. 24–25) take this issue further. They argue in favor of starting not only from broad social contexts but also from "the institutional location, the social relations of the texts and social practices within which literacy practices are embedded." This starting point is useful because whatever academic achievement is, it is certainly deeply institutional. After all, the basic structure of getting grades can be found in colleges and universities from Hanoi to Barcelona to MSU.

This understanding forces us to appreciate the fact that the Design of academic literacy can never really mimic that of any professional environment, as the notion of "authentic pedagogy" would imply. A business class can never be a business because it has different "social motives," as Freedman and her colleagues (Freedman and Medway 1994; Freedman, Adam, and Smart 1994) have pointed out. Similarly, learning in formal education can never be the same as learning outside. What happens in a classroom will never match the ideal of spontaneous learning outside because education takes place in institutions that have to respond to the requirements of many different stakeholders. These may include various combinations of teachers, trustees, prospective employers of graduates, students, administrators, politicians, and taxpayers, whose agendas may conflict or be in symbiosis, but in any case need to be addressed.

NOT READING BUT STILL KIND OF EXPECTING AN "A"

So far, my goals in this introduction have been to specify the overall problem and describe the general theoretical framework. One more task is to indicate and then justify the selection of the focus, which is the analysis of information and its management in academic settings. I use the word "justify" because an informational focus will probably be seen by some readers as opposed to important trends in academic literacy research, particularly those that assume a social perspective. So in this section, I will explain how information became the central object of this work and why its selection in no way contradicts the social viewpoint.

In fact, as is frequent in qualitative research (Merriam 1988), this focus was not the one that I had in mind in the beginning of this study. Initially, my idea was far more traditional—to examine the academic literacy of the case-study students from the point of view of their reading processes. One motive for this attention to reading was that most work within the socioliteracy tradition on higher education has focused on writing (e.g., Horowitz 1986; Walvoord and McCarthy 1990; Chiseri-Strater 1991; Johns 1991; Leki 1995; among many others). Yet as Johns (1991, 1997) and Spack (1997) have suggested, reading has frequently proved be a more important factor in educational achievement than writing. A little reflection shows that this is hardly a surprising finding. There are many college classes that require little or no writing, but almost all assign substantial amounts of reading. Thus, it seemed worthwhile to address this imbalance.

However, only a few weeks of research were required to make clear that however compelling this approach seemed in principle, it was not going to be as fruitful as I had hoped. The participants reported reading sporadically and inconsistently. Worse, the assiduousness of their reading was not in any obvious way related to their achievement. Greg, the case-study participant with the highest GPA, sold his statistics textbook within two weeks of buying it. Carmin, the one with the next highest GPA, never even bothered to buy her "required" Introduction to Theatre text. In her other classes, she did buy her books, but her reading was so sporadic that in the last interview she admitted to being "embarrassed to come in here and talk to you guys sometimes without having done any reading and still kinda expecting to get an A." By painful contrast, the two participants with lower GPAs, Sophie and Will, read more of what was assigned to them, though nowhere near all. Furthermore, only Will—the one who was least successful!—actually made consistent efforts to understand what he decided to read.

Although it is perfectly possible that I had simply been unlucky in my selection of participants, there was reason to believe that they were not atypical in their inconsistent reading, at least at MSU. First, two of the participants' teachers admitted that the "required" reading in their classes was not actually necessary for achieving good grades but was more of a resource for students who did not get the information for whatever reason from the lecture or recita tion.[3] One of them, Will's International Relations professor, reported that if he organized his course in such a way that reading were really necessary, the results would be catastrophic for the students' grades. In his words, "Students don't read; they can't read; they don't want to read; and they don't get as much out of it" as they do from oral language.

Even when faculty did insist that students read, their ways of enforcing their determination showed just how marginal reading could be. For example, Carmin's theatre professor was resolute that students read the plays being studied, which were purchased individually. However, she was so worried that many would not otherwise do so that she had the teaching assistants give quizzes in recitation on the factual content of each play. To make sure they read *Oedipus Rex*, for example, the professor asked students in Carmin's recitation section to supply the hero's mother's name, his birthplace, and the name of the oracle that predicted the events of the play. Such a quiz had little to do with assessing students' knowledge; instead it was a transparent tool for controlling their behavior. The professor also harbored, correctly, as was clear from Carmin's decision not to buy the textbook, doubts that they would voluntarily read much of the theoretical material the book contained, so she announced in the syllabus that exams would contain questions requiring information from the book that would not be touched on in the lectures. Even though Carmin had been warned about this enforcement mechanism, she still did not purchase the textbook. She had been told by friends who had previously taken the course that it would be easy to figure out all of the relevant "missing" information. Her decision turned out to be a miscalculation since she was not able to recover this supposedly "obvious" content.

I do not want to overstate the case. As Carmin's plight shows, no student could possibly have done well without some reading. Nevertheless, reading was clearly not central to the academic achievement process of these students. Instead it was one of a number of tools they used to access information, and perhaps knowing when not to use this tool was helpful in achievement. In sum, it seems best to think of academic input as multimodal, including oral, written, and pictorial sources of information that interact sometimes in complex ways.

This marginality of reading and its integration with other information sources meant that maintaining the focus on the role of reading would have cut the data against the grain if I wished to understand processes of academic achievement. I would not have created a coherent set of findings but one in which certain data would be included because reading was in some way involved, kind of a technicality. Of course, I could also have examined a question about just reading, but the answer to this question would still involve multimodality since decisions of when to read and when not to read depended in many cases on the availability of the information in other formats. So I asked myself, why beat around the bush? Why not interrogate that multimodality directly? Or better, why not look beyond the mode, to the information that the various modes were encoding?

This decision led to a further evolution of my views because it became apparent that respondents' decisions were not only pushed by the nature or quantity of the incoming information from classes and readings. They were also being pulled by the anticipated destinations of the information, which included whatever they had to produce for a grade, including exams, essays, exercises, and oral presentations. For one thing, there was always too much incoming information for them to manage without some form of triage, and the sorting was typically made in terms of what they thought they would need. Furthermore, much of the information they did need had to be puzzled out in some way, and these puzzles were also resolved in terms of what they thought they would have to show on assessments.

After a difficult couple of weeks of worrying about where my study was going, I stood back and reflected on what I was seeing *as a whole*. From this effort to see the entire forest and not focus on the trees, it dawned on me that I was facing a complex system of information flows. Information moved from source through the student to an assessment of some kind. On this view, students appeared to be both channels and channellers of information, choosing and directing its flow from a source, through themselves, to a destination. That destination, an assessment instrument of some kind, served as a kind of information display, the result of which was a grade.

This view is hardly an internal cognitive one. On the contrary, this pattern of flows was constructed and negotiated by students, faculty, administration, and the larger society together. It is the system by which learning is enforced (Laurillard 1987) and credentialed, and so it is also the means by which students participate in the gatekeeping processes that college courses perform. Furthermore, as I will discuss in more detail later, this structure turned out to be inevitable and universal. It is not limited to fact-driven courses but included those that taught abstract concepts and procedures. Nor, it has been shown, is it limited to classes following a transmission pedagogy, but it is equally valid for those using implicit instruction (e.g., Freedman, Adam, and Smart 1994).

AN INFORMATIONAL STANCE

The switch in focus meant adopting what Devlin and Rosenberg (1996) call an "informational stance" toward the phenomena under study and led to a need to understand the phenomenon of information better. So I turned to a qualitative theory of information called situation theory (Barwise and Perry 1983; Devlin 1991, 1997) that I was familiar with from linguistics. The result is admittedly somewhat of a departure for literacy research, which has typically looked for its foundation in other areas, such as social, psychological, or semiotic theories.

Yet the choice was a useful one. As the analysis proceeded, I found it was possible to describe in detail patterns of information flows and classification of information types that were important factors in determining these flows. The result is a kind of informational pragmatics (similar to *linguistic* pragmatics but leaving out the requirement for language) of academic literacy, and a description of these patterns form the heart of the findings of this study. I argue that at least on one level these patterns constitute the Design of academic literacy.

The reader thus can expect a multicase literacy study that is recognizable in its roots but somewhat unusual in its focus. The usual suspects for theoretical grounding of academic literacy research (e.g., Bakhtin, Foucault, Vygotsky, or Halliday) are not absent, but they can be found only in the background. They explain the motivation for the patterns described and some of the forms of resistance and accommodation. In the foreground is a detailed analysis of a system of normatively Designed communication and interpretation, which is the way that students and faculty construct the pursuit of grades in college; it is their way of imposing an orderliness on this effort to make it comprehensible and predictable. It also resolves the competing demands of society, themselves, administration, and faculty as filtered through the institution of MSU. More specifically, students are seen as "situated artful actors" (Berkenkotter and Huckin 1995) with goals constrained by an ill-structured system governed by what we, in our role as faculty, consider assessments.

NOTES

1. It is learnable given, perhaps, the innate knowledge of an underlying template generative linguists call universal grammar, or general cognitive capacities as functionalists would have it. The dispute is immaterial to my point.

2. The importance of these issues can be seen in the computer world in the debate over open-source software. In the traditional commercial software model the code—the equivalent of the Design of the software—is neither emergent nor flexible. Thus, it is impossible to tell by using a commercial package (e.g., Windows) what the code is, and therefore that code is unavailable for modification if a bug is found or a new function is needed. Furthermore, most software producers keep the code as a closely guarded commercial secret. By contrast, in open-source software, such as Linux, the actual computer code is made available to users. Different software users can then modify it to fix bugs or better serve their specific purposes or tastes. As a result, an open-source software package is constantly evolving, and the package on one computer may very well be slightly different from the one another machine is running.

3. Recitation consists of sections of about thirty students from the larger lecture class who meet weekly with a teachng assistant for discussion.

Chapter 2

Where We Stand in the Field

INFORMATION AND ACADEMIC ACHIEVEMENT IN PREVIOUS RESEARCH

Although this is perhaps the first study to take an overtly informational stance in research on academic literacy, it is still possible to group studies in this area into four categories in terms of how they treat information, albeit implicitly. These categories roughly correspond to cognitively oriented research, rhetorically based research, genre studies, and comprehensive case studies. The first three classes respond to different orientations with ultimate disciplinary roots in psychology, literary interpretation, and linguistics, respectively. The fourth consists of studies that are only methodologically consistent, so there is overlap with the other three.

Information Flows in Cognitive Research

The closest to an overt concern with information can be found in cognitively oriented approaches. In fact, a distinguishing feature of cognitive science is its view of mental activity as a form of information processing. In education, therefore, work on studying and learning that takes a cognitive perspective usually looks at how students process information in their courses to understand how they learn it.

Much of this work consists of close examinations of particular strategies. These include note taking (e.g., Van Meter, Yokoi, and Pressley 1994), underlining (e.g., Peterson 1992), graphic organizers (reviewed in Dunston 1992), and various combinations (e.g.,

Thomas and Rower 1986; Schallert, Alexander, and Goetz 1988; Nist, Simpson, Olejnik, and Mealey 1991). Other researchers have looked at the role of reading comprehension of particular groups such as second language readers (e.g., Block 1986) and readers in compensatory programs (e.g., Steinberg, Bohning, and Choning 1991). Still others have examined studying in different ethnic and national populations for clues to cross-cultural variations in student outcomes (e.g., Robinson and Tayler 1989; Treisman 1992; Johansson and Jonsson 1996).

Another subset looks at the effects of students' attitudes on their studying and learning. These predispositions are of two kinds. The first relates to students' understanding of knowledge or epistemics (e.g., Walters 1990; Langer 1992; Alexander and Dochy 1994; Hammer 1994; Schommer 1994; Wineburg 1997). The second involves motivation (e.g., Nolen 1988; Pintrich and Garcia 1991, 1994; Pintrich and Shrauben 1992; Pintrich, Marx, and Boyle 1993; Schutz 1994; Boekaerts 1995).

It is interesting to examine the assumptions regarding information flows in this line of research, what might be called the basic informational Design, or "macrodesign," that they assume. Anderson and Armbruster (1984, p. 657) define the goal of studying as "getting the information from the written page into the student's head." Indeed, most of these works explore how this flow of information from classes and readings into a student's long-term memory is affected by various activities that are either strategically employed or the result of external or internal factors of various sorts. This is true irrespective of whether the flow is understood as direct (i.e., from page or lecture to student) or as the result of an active (re)construction on the part of the student of the material to be learned. This assumption leads to a definition of success, one that is so simple it appears to be largely unstated: Improvements involve becoming more proficient at learning more and higher-order information.

All these assumptions make sense considering the disciplinary focus of cognitive science on mental activity combined with the evident interest of educators in learning, and this coherence explains continuing influence of this research on educational practice. This productivity has led in turn to efforts to examine this issue from the student's perspective and to classify responses to course information into categories of practices that they use. An important example is Weinstein and Meyer's (1986, 1991) three-way taxonomy of learning strategies. These include (1) *repetition* or *rehearsal strategies* that lead to the acquisition of basic knowledge, (2) *elaboration strategies* that build bridges between new and old knowledge, and (3) *organization strategies* that involve transformations of knowledge into different forms. Rehearsal strategies may be considered the lowest order because they involve only the most basic form of knowledge. Organization strategies, by contrast, involve the highest-order thinking skills, and elaboration strategies fall somewhere in between.

Another influential distinction is Marton and Säljö's (1976) division of students' responses to course information into *deep-level* and *surface-level* processing. This distinction depends on students' goals in studying and the amount of thought involved in particular studying procedures. Entwistle (1984, 1987) elaborated Marton and Säljö's insights into what he called deep and surface "approaches." In this way he connects strategy research with the work on epistemics and motivation.

For Entwistle, a surface approach is characterized by simple completion of task requirements, memorization, conflation of principles and examples, a view of tasks as impositions, a focus on discrete bits of information, and a lack of reflection. By contrast, a deep approach consists of a desire to understand. This involves an active interaction with content, including relating new and old information, connecting abstractions to everyday experience, relating evidence and conclusions, and a consequent focus on the logic of an argument. Although Entwistle does not make the connection, this view suggests a reflection of these strategies in teaching approaches. A surface approach by a student corresponds to explicit instruction by a teacher, while a deep approach can be associated with implicit instruction. What is crucial here is to remember that the use of implicit instruction or a deep approach does not alter the gross pattern of information flow since the information still begins at a source (i.e., the curriculum) and ends at a target (i.e., the student's head), as described in Figure 2.1. What is different is how it gets there and probably what gets there. In the case of the deep approach, the student recreates the conceptual structures, but in the surface approach he or she merely copies them.

Figure 2.1
Surface or Deep Approaches

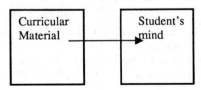

Entwistle (1987) adds a third approach called the *strategic approach*. Students using this approach attempt to obtain the highest possible grades through efficient organization of time, effort, study conditions, and materials. They also use grade-maximizing stratagems such as reviewing previous exams and paying attention to cues concerning assessment. The instructional mirror of this approach is measurement-driven instruction, or more prosaically, "teaching to the test."

Note that in the strategic approach, the assumptions regarding information flows differ from those in the rest of the cognitive literature. Here the information flows from material *through* the student to the assessor. In Figure 2.2 this flow is shown as a kind of information recycling because both the deliverer of the curricular material and the assessor are probably the same person, the instructor or, at minimum, the assessor who works in close contact with the instructor.

Within a strategic approach, the student's role is to select and direct this flow; the student is, as I describe it in Chapter 1, a channel and a channeller, not necessarily a repository. The all-important return flow takes the form of what I called an "information display" on an assessment instrument in the previous chapter. Therefore, while the first two approaches are about learning, the strategic approach is concerned with academic achievement. Whether the information stays in the student's head after it is delivered to the assessor is immaterial, as it indeed is to the student who takes a final exam in a course that is of no interest. Of course, as Pintrich and Garcia (1991) point out, the two approaches are not mutually exclusive. As entirely different ways of responding to course material, it is possible to achieve and learn simultaneously.

The addition of the strategic approach was made in response to the work of Laurillard (1984, 1987) and Hounsell (1984), who ques-

Figure 2.2
Strategic Approach

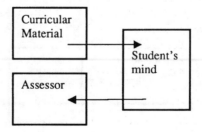

tion what they see as a pervasive conflation of learning and academic achievement in the literature on education and cognition. They argue that the equation of students' success with their learning and the concomitant assumption that the purpose of assessment is to measure the material learned are hopelessly naive. The problem might be thought of as the educational counterpart of the observer's paradox or the uncertainty principle in physics. Only it is not primarily an issue for researchers, but rather it pervades the educational system. Without assessing, you cannot establish what students learn, but by assessing you change what they learn.

It should be noted that such concerns about assessment effects are not new, at least outside cognitive educational research. The same case was made a long time before Laurillard by sociologists such as Becker, Geer, and Hughes (1968) and Miller and Partlett (1974). A similar distrust of the equation of learning with academic achievement continues independently in a number of studies right until the present (Crooks 1988; Robinson and Tayler 1989; Nelson 1990; Thorkildsen and Nicholls 1991; Hill and Parry 1989, 1992, 1994; Wineburg 1997; Mann 2000). Gordon and Hanauer (1995, p. 317) neatly describe the assessment task as "an additional information source" that is used by the test taker in the construction of a mental model of the task. That information source makes it a task different from learning.

Laurillard's case is particularly intriguing because her claims are the strongest and are made from within the cognitive tradition. She argues that cognitive studies of learning are *inherently* (though not hopelessly) problematic in educational contexts. Their difficulty comes from the fact that human cognition is designed for learning that takes place in natural environments, such as the social and physical contexts in which it has evolved. Academics, however, is an unnatural environment.

The natural and the unnatural environment are distinguished by the fact that the former provides knowledge of the world, the latter provides knowledge of descriptions of the world. It is the difference between perceptual knowledge (of the physical world) and what I choose to call 'preceptual' knowledge (of the theoretical world). It is the knowledge of *pre*cepts that gives us so much trouble, and is what concerns educationalists. What makes them difficult is that they are not afforded to us in the way that *per*cepts are. (Laurillard 1987, pp. 200–201)

The unnatural *preceptual* nature of learning in an educational environment, Laurillard argues, leads to the structure of teaching and grading that characterizes these environments. What we refer to as assessments do not even mainly function to assess learning.

Rather these practices serve primarily as ways of fostering certain behaviors; their purpose is to direct students "to look at the physics book rather than go to the movies" (Laurillard 1987, p. 204). However, because of the rewards and punishments used as incentives, the content being learned as a product of those mechanisms is crucially not the curricular material but the means of academic achievement, such as how to pass a test. On this view what appears paradoxical (i.e., the observer effect) is actually the point.

Information Flows in Rhetorical Research

Laurillard may overstate the case—surely students do not only learn how to pass tests; nor is motivation the only purpose of assessments. However, she is hardly alone in understanding education in terms of social processes related to control of students. This outlook is characteristic of much of the literature on academic literacy done from a rhetorical perspective, in which I would group both Critical (e.g., Benesch 1995) and Process (e.g., Raimes 1985) tendencies. An example is Bartholomae and Petrosky's (1988) account of a program designed to aid struggling students, which has elements of both. These authors blame a structure of academic literacy that is too focused on information for the problems their students face. They see this focus as leading to a process by which academic literacy is constructed as a shuttling of facts from teacher or text to student and back again to the teacher. This is of course nothing other than the structure delineated by Entwistle's "strategic approach." Bartholomae and Petrosky argue that this process is culturally alien to many students.[1] They propose that the way out of the resulting cycle of failure is the adoption of a "pedagogy of counterfactuality," which replaces the information shuttling with creativity and critique. They wish to encourage students to produce textual artifacts that respond to and challenge the facts they are exposed to and so focus on creative engagement with content rather than information.

There are thus evident parallels between Bartholomae and Petrosky's socially and rhetorically driven critique and Laurillard's cognitive one. Nevertheless, they find different origins for the problem. For Laurillard it is inherent in education, lying in the *preceptual* nature of the material to be learned and educators' consequent deployment of "artificial devices" (Laurillard 1987, p. 207), such as tests, to encourage learning. Bartholomae and Petrosky less pessimistically find the problem in what they consider poor pedagogy. Use of their "pedagogy of counterfactuality" with its roots in critical literacy and process writing will presumably make learning more successful by eliminating the recycling. Students will produce new information and real communication will take place.

Nevertheless, a closer look reveals that this pedagogy does not, in fact, change the structure of the information flows. Bartholomae and Petrosky's claim that it does rests on a number of fallacies, the first of which is that the information recycled is simply facts. This is an easy error to make because no one would argue that each *individual piece of information* learned is not factual (or better, propositional) in format (Barwise and Perry 1983; Kruglanski 1989). Yet these pieces do not come independent of each other, and they are not meant to be taught, learned, or recycled, for that matter, in isolation.

Instead, information forms schemata that are more than the sum of their component propositional parts. In Weinstein and Meyer's (1986, 1991) organization strategies, the structure of connections is what is being organized. In Entwistle's deep approach the structures are what lie below the surface. The reason that they have to be organized and dug up is that they cannot be simply memorized because they involve too many individual pieces simultaneously. By the same token, the expression of the structure is also typically implicit in the sense that a writer of a textbook or student on an exam may communicate it indirectly. The reader or grader must often infer it for reasons that will be discussed in detail in Chapter 6.

Bartholomae and Petrosky's second fallacy is the same one that Laurillard accused her fellow cognitive researchers of assuming, the conflation of learning and academic achievement. Bartholomae and Petrosky claim that by following their proposals, students will learn better, and presumably this will be reflected on assessments. Yet they do not in fact change the basic recycling structure, only what is being recycled. In the pedagogy of counterfactuality—as in every other pedagogy—the production of artifacts and their content by students is still stimulated in some sense by instructors through assignments and readings. Similarly, whenever there is assessment, there is a rubric—tacit or concrete—according to which certain features found in student work (e.g., an essay) trigger specific points. Standard grammar, critical stance to a reading, rhetorical organization, and even creativity are potential features that gain points. Those target, or what I call *criterial,* features are in and of themselves treated as information showing the students' progress, and so the assignment constitutes and is treated as an information display. In the case of an essay *the criterial information*—what an assignment is really communicating—is again rarely if ever its propositional contents. Instead, it is what those contents imply about the writer's command of the instructional objectives of the course.

The inevitability of this recycling pattern was captured best by Trimbur (1994, p. 110). This critic referred to students in a process-oriented writing class in the following way: "The canniest among them recognized that sincerity and authenticity of voice were the privileged terms of symbolic exchange." In sum, while it is tempting to believe that placing sincerity and authenticity in the curriculum somehow fundamentally changes the basic Design, these changes are less profound than they appear.

Genre Approaches

A social approach is more solidly founded in work on genre (Mehan 1980; Swales 1990; Briggs and Baumann 1992; Kress 2000; Freedman and Medway 1994; Berkenkotter and Huckin 1995; Johns 1997). An individual's learning is understood as a function of their integration into academic discourse communities (e.g., Swales 1990; Chimbganda 2000) or communities of practice (Lave and Wenger 1991). A discourse community is understood in terms of a sharing of language features, including grammar, pragmatic norms, and content of texts used for some set of community purposes over time. Communities of practice are similar though somewhat both smaller, because they are typically more local, and broader, because they mix linguistic with other communicative and noncommunicative functions. They are defined as goal-oriented groups characterized by such features as frequent interactions, shared communicative norms, markers of membership, and defined identities. In such communities, novices learn by a kind of apprenticeship called "legitimate peripheral participation," leading to subsequent full participation. A successful student is one who acts more and more as a member of the community that the class is preparing for.

Besides showing the diverse goals students have, this type of research has given a sense of the importance of genre, which is understood as social action in a variety of domains. The domains include reading (Carson et al. 1992; Haas 1994; Spack 1997), writing (Walvoord and McCarthy 1990; Johns 1991; Leki 1995; Berkenkotter and Huckin 1995), oral presentations (Freedman, Adam, and Smart 1994), and testing (e.g., Gordon and Hanauer 1995). Other work has shown the importance and nature of such factors as expertise in the subject matter (Geisler 1994), cultural differences (Spack 1997), and epistemic preferences (Hammer 1994; Alexander and Dochy 1994; Simpson and Nist 1997).

Classes based on this view tend to support the use of pedagogies that inculcate socialization into professional or academic communities through apprenticeship-like experiences and so rely on simulations of the types of discourse and situations to be encountered in these communities. Assessments in such classes therefore take naturalistic formats, typically performances or samples of work (Berkenkotter and Huckin 1995). Again, as in the case of cognitive studies, this has proved a productive position given the concerns with and the importance of social and linguistic factors in students' growth, persistence, and development.

Yet just as Laurillard and others have challenged the equivalence of academic achievement and learning on cognitive grounds, some genre and writing researchers have expressed doubts concerning the equivalence of academic achievement to community of practice membership. Freedman, Adam, and Smart (1994), for instance, discuss the different "social motives" between classroom and noneducational communities. For all the attempts to simulate professional environments, a classroom remains subject to specifically educational communicative strictures. The most important of these are assessments and the rewards and punishments that flow from them. As Freedman and colleagues (1994, p. 206) claim in a discussion of the writing of students in a business course, "Their writing was governed by the need not just to provide appropriate arguments but, more significantly, to prove *what* and *that* they knew. . . . How much detail to include, then, is not based on what readers need to know in order to make a decision or act but rather on what is necessary to demonstrate what the writer knows. *Student writing is the knowing made manifest* for inspection." Once again we find that, although some apprenticeship pedagogues may also believe that they have short-circuited the informational recycling patterns characteristic of fact-based explicit instruction, students realize that this change is superficial. They only succeed in making their information displays more complex and indirect, as Trimbur notes. Similarly, Johns (1997, p. 151) points to the limits of applying any kind of professional community integration model to undergraduate writing: "Many of the students enrolled in our literacy classes and our universities do not aspire to be fully initiated members of disciplinary communities or devote their lives to academic study. Instead, they have chosen to go into business, computer technology, engineering, and other professions." These arguments, like Laurillard's, lead to an understanding of academic settings as, while not unnatural, at least ones with their own communicative strictures that cannot be assimilated to noneducational environments. Academic achievement involves learning, but it cannot be reduced to cognitive processes; it involves operating according to new social norms, but it is not only social integration.

All this is not to imply that all forms of assessment are equal and portfolios or performances are not worthwhile. Each way of assessing certainly has different pedagogical effects, and therefore different methods will better support different instructional objectives. However, these critiques imply that terms like "authentic assessment" are misleading in two ways. First, no form of educational assessment is authentic in the sense that it is used in what students sometimes call "the real world" because the context and social motives will always be specific to the classroom. A law student, for example, gets an A; a lawyer wins a case and gets a fee. The lawyer gets the fee because his solution worked or the firm's profits grew. The student gets an A because her brief contained all the elements that the law professor expected, although these may have been as flexible and abstract as "flawless logic" or "creativity." The only exception is when the law student is actually helping in a real case, and this exception proves the rule since the student has moved beyond the classroom.

The notion of authentic assessment is also misleading because it implies that other forms of educational assessment are somehow "unreal." But educational contexts are all genuine in the sense that people create them, participate in them, and are affected by them. They are different from their professional or noneducational equivalents in the same way that a game is different from any phenomenon it might appear to simulate. Yet "authentic assessments" do not eliminate this game-like nature—they can only disguise it.

Information Flows in Case-Study Research

The research that most consistently articulates social and cognitive issues consists of comprehensive case-study examinations of students (e.g., Haas 1994; Spack 1997) or courses (e.g., Walvoord and McCarthy 1990; Carson, Chase, Gibson, and Hargrove 1992; Greene 1993; Freedman, Adam, and Smart 1994; Hammer 1994; Simpson and Nist 1997). The authors of these works may take a rhetorical, genre, or cognitive perspective, or some combination, and so overlap with these viewpoints. However, the shared research methodology forces certain commonalities in their understanding of what students do with information.

Haas (1994) and Spack (1997), for example, show undergraduates who exhibited characteristics of Entwistle's "deep approach," trying to understand and assimilate what they read. At the same time, their epistemic orientation and thinking about literate activity became increasingly assimilated to more advanced, if not discipline-specific, discursive practices. On the other hand, they simultaneously maintained an assessment-oriented "strategic approach."

Similar findings can be found in case studies of courses and classes. Carson and colleagues (1992) in the study of a high-attrition history class point out how studying is directed and shaped from the very beginning by the assessment instruments that ultimately end the process. They can also be found in the conclusions reached by a cognitive study by Simpson and Nist (1997) who combine a case study of a class with close analyses of selected students in that class. They again show that a combination of strategic and deep approaches was characteristic of high achievement. Simpson and Nist paint success as a product of adaptability to circumstances and an awareness of academic demands—strategies appropriate for ill-structured problems—rather than consistent use of particular discursive practices. Finally, Berkenkotter and Huckin (1995, p. ix) also anticipate certain proposals made here including the classification of students as "situated artful actors whose acts of communication occur within semiotic systems," as I stated in Chapter 1.

Taken together, these studies imply that information recycling as described by Entwistle's "strategic approach" is nothing less than what I earlier called the macrodesign of academic achievement. It follows that knowledge of the characteristics of these flows and the information that composes them will provide the researcher with better understanding of why students get the grades they do. This better understanding is also likely to be a useful tool for students who wish to do better and for faculty who wish to develop forms of the recycling—since the pattern is inevitable—that best mesh with their instructional goals. Yet in research on higher education, study skills, or academic literacy, the Design of information flows or academic information itself has not yet been the object of research attention.

One probable reason for this absence is that academic literacy has traditionally involved the application of theories and paradigms taken from other disciplines, such as cognitive science, rhetoric, or linguistics; and each has looked at academic literacy through its own disciplinary lens. Therefore, educational psychologists have looked at academic literacy in terms of cognitive processing. Rhetoricians have looked at it as composition, ultimately borrowing their theoretical paradigm from literary interpretation. Linguists have tended to look at academic literacy in terms of genre. The absence of an informational perspective may be traced to the fact that information theorists have not examined literacy, and that educators of all stripes have not learned information theory.

INFORMATION THEORY

One reason that educators lack interest in information theory may be that on first impression it just does not seem to be an appropriate tool. Most information theorists are concerned with the efficient movement of quantities of information, for example, through computer networks. Their work therefore has a quite different set of applications, ones that seem utterly unsuitable for an investigation of how humans, rather than automated systems, interact with information. Computers, for example, are notoriously bad at solving ill-structured problems. Yet the definition of information used in this theory, based on a seminal insight by Shannon (1948–1949) (cited in Dretske 1981), points the way to a softer, more human understanding. This idea relates to the situated nature of information that is needed to quantify it.

Imagine a job hunter who hears that he is one of sixty-four applicants for a position. Later, in spite of these low odds he happily receives the call that he has been selected as one of four finalists who will be interviewed. This information can be quantified *in terms of a reduction in uncertainty* as to who will get the job. The method of quantification itself is of doubtful relevance to the understanding of information in academic achievement.[2] I do not see academic literacy as measuring information flows into students' heads or even through them to assessment instruments. Still, the notion of reduction of uncertainty itself reveals an important characteristic of information that is relevant. It means that the information the candidate received was quantifiable only because he was one of sixty-four candidates and he already knew it. In other words, the information was neither "out there," say, in the message he received (e.g., "you have been selected as one of our four finalists") nor in the objective fact of his having first been one of sixty-four. It was not even in his head in how he processed the message. Instead it was simultaneously a function of both the objective facts and his understanding of those facts. Information, it seems, is inherently *situated*. Indeed, situation theory (Barwise and Perry 1983; Barwise 1986/1988; Devlin 1991, 1997), which developed out of Dretske's observations, has been cited as the philosophical foundation for situated cognition (Greeno and Moore 1993). It has been used in a wide variety of areas, including linguistics (Pollard and Sag 1994; Barlow 1992; Newman 1998), communication analysis (Devlin and Rosenberg 1996), artificial intelligence (Israel and Perry 1991), and logic (Barwise and Echemendy 1990).

Situated or distributed cognition differs from traditional or symbolic views in that it distributes cognition between internal symbolic manipulations and external constraints (e.g., Rumelhart and Norman 1988; Norman 1990, 1993; Zhang and Norman 1994. See also the debate between Vera and Simon 1993 and Greeno and Moore 1993). In education it is best known for its use in support of a cognitive apprenticeship model of learning (e.g., Brown, Collins, and Duguid 1989). As such, it is part of what Gee calls the "social turn" in cognition. Nevertheless, this is not precisely the same sense as that used in theories influenced by Marxist sociology (e.g., Lave and Wenger 1991), although there is some confusion about this and other facets in some educational research. For example, Norman and colleagues do not claim that there is one type of cognition that is situated and another that is nonsituated, as Berkenkotter and Huckin (1995, p. 11) imply in their discussion of genre knowledge as "a form of situated cognition." Instead, for these authors situatedness is a characteristic of even nonhuman cognition.

My goal here is to begin to apply some tools of situation theory to educational communication, in particular its semantic powers. The semantics constitutes a formal logic of information that differs from classic formal logics—such as those in the Russellian or Fregean traditions—most basically in the use of the notion of situation to account for context (see Devlin 1997). A situation is any portion of reality that is not treated atomically but as structured or at least decomposible to smaller parts: "A *situation* can be thought of as a limited part of reality. Such parts may have spatio-temporal extent, or they may be more abstract, such as fictional worlds, context of utterance, problem domains, mathematical structures, databases, Unix directories, and various other possibilities" (Devlin and Rosenberg 1996, p. 21). The core of situation theory is the idea that information arises from regularities—referred to as *uniformities*—across *situations*. This idea is realized in the relation theory of meaning, defined as follows:

One situation *s* can contain information about another situation *s'* only if there is a systematic relation *M* that holds between situations sharing some configuration of uniformities with *s* and some other configuration of uniformities with *s'*. These uniformities may be physical objects, abstract objects like words, physical or abstract properties or relations, places, or times, or other uniformities. . . . But in any case, it is the relationship *M* that allows us to say that the first situation means the second. (Barwise and Perry 1983, p. 14)

Examples of these systematic relations include products of natural laws (e.g., *smoke means fire*), conventional relations (e.g., *a fire alarm means fire*), and linguistic conventions (e.g., *"FIRE" means fire*). The theory provides a way of modeling the *orderliness* in these relations between situations under the assumption that it is this order that enables cognitive agents to extract and use information.

As applied to this study, this viewpoint places a familiar set of understandings in a new light. It would see students as cognitive agents who make sense of their classes by finding abstract uniformities and patterns of such uniformities in the material they are given. They look, to give just one example, for similarities and differences within and across classes and texts and between the information they find in a class and that outside of that class, including in previous knowledge. These relations between uniformities constitute the course information. They are the material students work with.

On this view, a class can be seen as a kind of virtual environment that students make their way through. Just as any living being uses the information available in the environment to survive, so students have to identify the relevant factors in the abstract environment of ideas of a class. Just as there is too much information available in a real environment, so in a classroom a student must triage the information, discarding what will not be useful. Just as in a real environment there are underlying patterns that cannot be immediately perceived, so in a classroom the essential information may not lie visibly on the surface.

Importantly, potentially useful information may remain invisible to many students or even to whole classes or categories of students. The same is true in the natural environment. One striking example in nature involves lions. These animals are five times more successful when they attack prey from downwind than when they attack from upwind because from downwind the prey cannot smell them before they see them. Yet lions attack as often from upwind as downwind. Information that may be of life and death value to them is available in the environment, but they are incapable of processing it. So it is that a clueless student may have the information available but continue looking in the wrong place, following old habits time after time after time.

Yet there is more involved in the student's virtual environment than the information that composes it. There is also what students must do with it, which I described in the previous section as being one of recycling for a grade. Information theory can also help us understand those flows. Even before the development of situation theory, the situated nature of information was used by Dretske (1981) to develop a theory of how information can flow. Dretske makes three important observations concerning the nature of these flows. The first explains how educational (and other) communication is possible at all; the other two act as qualifications of particular importance to educational contexts. They explain both constraints on flows and their propensity to produce unintended consequences. The first of these observations is what Dretske (1981, p. 57) calls the Xerox Principle, for the photocopier metaphor that elegantly illustrates it:

If *A* carries the information that *B,* and *B* carries the information that *C,* then *A* carries the information that *C.*

It is this property that allows information to flow—that permits the same information to appear in a lecture, in a student's notes, and then on a test. However, this simple process is qualified by the fact that signals (writing on paper, configurations of electrons in a phone line, or linguistic constructions) do not carry only one piece of information:

It makes little sense . . . to speak of the informational content of a signal as though this was unique. Generally speaking, a signal carries a great variety of different informational contents, a great variety of different pieces of information, and although these pieces of information may be related to each other (e.g., logically), they are nonetheless *different* pieces of information. (Dretske 1981, p. 72)

For example, a student on a test writes a fact (e.g., Napoleon founded the Bank of France) that was originally encountered in a lecture or textbook, or selects that fact from a set of multiple-choice possibilities. That response does not only or even primarily contain the propositional information thus expressed. It provides information about everything logically embedded or "nested" (Devlin 1991) in that information. Most prominently, an assumption of a test maker must be that the production or selection of that response indicates the student's *knowledge* that Napoleon founded the Bank of France. Our confidence in what an item on a test measures is the validity of the item.

However, it is here that the system meets a snag. In an assessment instrument, this confidence can only be partial if for no other reason that the student may have guessed.[3] Yet even if the validity were perfectly well grounded, there is more to be said. The ability to reproduce a fact or collection of facts may embed other information. For example, how the student arranges facts, say, on an essay test, may imply an understanding of important connections between those facts. So a student who lists many of Napoleon's legal and economic reforms shows an understanding of that leader as a modernizing force. That student may therefore gain points for that more abstract knowledge in addition to the facts presented in contrast to a classmate who simply lists facts about Napoleon's reign haphazardly. However, the grader may also expect a student to state directly that "Napoleon was a modernizing force" to gain other points (e.g., for knowledge of academic writing conventions that require explicitness). In this case the knowledge of the classification of

Napoleon as a modernizer is both implicit—in the listing of modernizations—and explicit in the statement. Here only the adherence to the generic norms is implicit.

There is also other implicit information embedded in the essay test. These include how much studying the student did, whether he or she conforms to the ideology implicit in schooling, and so on. So the recycling of a fact or set of facts or concepts contains a great deal more information than just the reproducer's knowledge of those facts or concepts, or paradoxically, if we have doubts about the item's validity, perhaps a lot less.

The third principle further qualifies the process as outlined above, and it could be understood as the source of how assessment fundamentally shapes the educational process—the observer effect I mentioned in the introduction:

> We cannot use [an] instrument simultaneously to collect information about [what it is measuring] and about its own reliability. . . . The same phenomenon is illustrated when we "test" a friend about whom we have become suspicious. We ask him to tell us about a situation of which we are already informed. His response tells us (gives us information) about *him,* not about the situation he is (perhaps accurately) describing. (Dretske 1981, p. 117)

I have already briefly mentioned this issue with respect to item validity, but the test is not the only channel. As Dretske's citation makes clear, *humans can be channels of information.* As I said in the introduction, students are channels because they act as a human *conveyer* of information relating to curricular objectives. The student conveys these facts, concepts, critical thinking, and/or genre norms from some source (e.g., lecture, reading, class discussion, video) to some assessment (e.g., test, paper, exercise, oral presentation). Note that it would be considered unfair to grade students on something that we have not provided in some way, however indirectly. However, as in the case of the person of whom we are suspicious, the information that assessors *really want* is not the content the student is trying to convey, which we already know. The assessors are using that content, like the person who suspects the other, only as a tool to find out information about the student.

From an informational stance, educational communication thus looks extremely complex, consisting of various levels, six of which are illustrated in Table 2.1, although they could conceivably be stretched further. In each exam, paper, exercise, or oral presentation, it is possible that the information actually being communicated can be found at any level, or more than one level, besides the one labeled "propositional content." In most cases, the information

Table 2.1
Levels of Information in Educational Communication

Level	Signal employed	Information	example
Propositional content	a sentence in an essay, a multiple choice item, statement in an oral presentation, etc.	Propositional content	"Napoleon founded the Bank of France."
Embedded information 1	a sentence in an essay, multiple choice item, oral presentation, etc	student knows propositional content	"Student knows that Napoleon founded the Bank of France."
Embedded information 2	content together with other items, whole essay, etc.	Student knows schemata	"Student knows that Napoleon modernized the state."
Embedded information 3	content together with other items, whole essay, etc	Student knows concepts	"Student knows about enlightenment and its effects."
Embedded information 4	content together with other items, whole essay, etc	Student knows generic norms	"Student knows about how to organize academic writing."
Embedded information 5	content together with other items, whole essay, etc	implications regarding how student got this knowledge	"Student studied for exam."
Embedded information 6	content together with other items, whole essay, etc	Implications about student's conformity to social norms	"Student at least acquiesces to the role assigned culturally to students in college."

at this "zero" level is already known by the instructor. A history professor presumably knows what Napoleon did; a chemistry professor is familiar with the notion of atomic weight, and a statistics professor understands everything about means, modes, and medians that a student can report. The lack of importance of this level can be seen on multiple-choice exams that are not even read but are corrected mechanically. Of course it could be objected that in some cases, such as in a writing class, this information may not be previously known to the instructor. However, these new contents, of a story, autobiography, or opinion, are not criterial. The features triggering the grade are more abstract and familiar to the grader, and they are embedded in this novel information. For example, two students could write on opposing sides of a controversial question and get the same grade. Alternatively, they could come up with essentially the same opinion, but the one whose paper presents more of the desired forms of argumentation and Standard English usage will achieve the higher grade.

As the levels of embedding get deeper and deeper, the communication gets more indirect and so more tentative and more complex. It is far more straightforward to indicate knowledge of facts than it is to indicate knowledge of concepts. However, the communication of facts is in and of itself superficial. To demonstrate that they control concepts such as "enlightenment" or "democracy," students must interpret facts in light of the concept. Such information is most easily expressed in extended prose. The interpretation of expression of knowledge of generic norms is even more complex, which is why writing assessment is so difficult.

However, even in the simplest cases, the communication of criterial information is potentially subtle and elaborate, and the frequently bizarre pragmatics associated with tests (Hill and Parry 1992, 1994; Hill and Larsen 2000) may stem from the complexity. It is certainly easy, as we will see in Part II, for students to become utterly confused about what professors expect on various forms of assessment.

Yet in spite of this difficulty, we unfortunately have not arrived at the final complicating factor. It is this: Students know they are being tested and are usually determined to do the best job they can of providing the information that is expected, whether they know it or not. It is as if Dretske's suspect were aware of his interlocutor's suspicion. Innocent or guilty, he has to try to give the questioner the information that she expects. Because students often cannot be entirely sure of what the expected content is, the process takes on a certain degree of guesswork. Furthermore, because of the stakes involved, there are certain efforts to create a system that can be accepted as minimally fair. Thus, there are rules and norms, such as "Don't copy someone else's work" for students, and "Don't ask questions on tests out of the blue" for teachers. Put together, this enormous complexity and ill structure resolves itself in the only way it can for humans—as a game-like system. The game consists of movements of pieces of information of various types made by students following strategic decisions that result in displays of the information. The displays trigger payoffs in the form of grades based on how much of the expected information they contain. I call this system "The Academic Achievement Game." In this study, my goal is to begin an exploration of this game and discover some of the principles by which it operates.

Finally, to close this section I have to admit that these points, however complicated, do not yet justify the adoption of an entirely new set of theoretical tools, with its associated costs of difficulties of comprehension for the uninitiated, a group that includes just about everyone in the field. I fear that I have already burdened readers with enough unfamiliar abstraction. Perhaps a better-known framework could provide enough insight to make the addition of yet another complicated set of concepts, such as those contained in situation theory, unnecessary. If a theory is a tool, why acquire a new one if an old one might do the job? Also, a more familiar theory would better serve to link my claims to the customary approaches to academic literacy and the questions they address. I admit that it is problematic to stray so far from familiar ground.

Yet what I will argue here is that the addition of new tools is necessary to understand just how this information game is played; no other better-established theory will do the job because no other theory is designed for the job. For example, other tools such as systemic linguistics, critical theory, and practice theory are discourse or sociologically based. They have proved invaluable in understanding the uses of discourse, power relations, and the role of human agency in shaping group identity and norms. So my arguments for the addition of situation-theoretic tools are simply that they provide a better understanding of an underexplored aspect of academic literacy: its contents and what happens to those contents as students use them to get grades. Furthermore, I am not arguing against these other approaches; the acceptance of theories is not a zero-sum game because there is nothing necessarily incompatible about them.

In any case, one contribution I will refer to in the next chapter leads us back to the lions and the wind. The insight is that the way organisms respond to their environment can be understood informationally. Each organism responds to reality using different schemata that determine the uniformities to which it is attuned. A lion does not learn to attack from downwind because it is not attuned to wind direction and cannot learn to become so attuned. When an organism responds systematically to a uniformity, such as wind direction, a place, or a type of organism, situation theorists say that it "discriminates" that uniformity. Some attunements, and so some discriminations, are not innate but are learned. So it is that humans and some more cognitively complex animals gain attunements to things of which they were not originally aware. So it also is that some patterns of attunements can take on cultural dimensions.

One aspect of higher cognition is the ability to *identify* a uniformity to which an agent is attuned; and in this case, situation theorists say that the agent individuates that uniformity. Thus a cat or dog appears to recognize a person it knows as an individual. In the case of humans, we typically apply names to those uniformities we individuate. Individuation, as opposed to mere discrimination, allows for greater precision and control. Humans individuate and discriminate not only uniformities in the world but also those that we create in our abstract social environment. So, for example, we individuate such uniformities as *sibling, lion,* and *danger.* In this study, we will be concerned with which *academic* uniformities the case-study students individuated and discriminated because their ability to do so appears to be an important factor in their success.

MULTILITERACIES

The existence of an information-based system would remain without conceptual attachment to literacy studies if it were not for the development of the New London Group's (1996/2000) concept of Design. I discussed the basics of Design in the introduction. Here, I will limit myself to filling out some of the details.

To begin at the beginning, Design is the solution to what is potentially a foundational crisis in literacy studies that arises from the difficulties of maintaining graphic language as defining literacy. Traditionally, of course, literacy found its material in the learning of reading and writing graphic representations of language (Goody and Watt 1968; Luria 1974/1976; Ong 1992). Yet several events coincided in making this original definition untenable. First, Scribner and Cole's (1981) classic study of vernacular literacy and its effects made clear that print itself was a lot less transcendent than had been originally thought. Instead, it was realized that *the uses of* reading and writing (Heath 1982, 1983) and how they were constructed socially (Street 1984; Erickson 1986) provided more insight into problems of learning and teaching. Yet this "socio-literacy" (Johns 1997) has left literacy research with a certain lack of focus (Hasan 1998). If print itself is not transcendent—as socioliteracy denies—then it becomes difficult to maintain even uses of reading and writing as defining a separate camp of study (Gee 1989; Newman forthcoming). Yet without print, where is the coherence? Literacy could study anything.

Second, the definition of "literacy" in popular use appears to be broadening with little input or help from the literacy theorists. Terms like "cultural literacy," "computer literacy," and "geographic literacy," which do not make reference to written language, have become current in the media and popular culture. While some literacy theorists (e.g., Snow and Dickinson 1991, p. 180) have argued that these usages reduce the meaning of literacy to "nothing more than skill, competence, or knowledge," a closer analysis reveals that these fears are unfounded. For example, computer literacy does not mean any knowledge about computers; a computer literate person does not need to know how to program computers or repair them. Similarly, geographic literacy does not mean knowing how to draw maps or even being familiar with what academic geographers study. Instead, "literacy" in these cases refers to a specific kind of competence, an ability to function with informational tools in the named domain, be it computers, geography, or something else. It is a kind of foundational knowledge of a communicative system and its elements necessary to work with that system in the domain specified.

Finally, it makes sense to think of this spontaneous evolution of the word "literacy" as responding to changes in the culture of communication. These changes began arguably with the appearance of the telegraph in the nineteenth century and have only accelerated as time has gone on. The result is that the role of print as the key form of information storage and transfer has declined in importance in favor of a more versatile and faster mix of media. It is possible to be nostalgic for the monopoly of the printed word. Alternately as it is possible to rejoice in the utopian possibilities of the information age. It is probably more useful, however, to start with technological change as a historical fact. If print is less important than it once was, it makes sense to look beyond traditional print-based notions of literacy. The alternative is to accept that literacy is a concept whose time is passing, but the sheer productivity of literacy studies argues against a scenario of decadence.

The contribution of the New London Group has been to retheorize literacy on the basis of where this productivity is most evident, which arguably involves genre (e.g., Swales 1990; Johns 1997) and the social nature of communication (e.g., Heath 1982; Cazden 1988; Gee 1991). Multiliteracies extends these contributions beyond print to the linguistic, spatial (e.g., architecture), visual (e.g., painting), auditory (e.g., music), gestural (e.g., dance), and multimodal (e.g., Web pages). It also refines and theorizes the flexible systematicity consistently noted by socioliteracy researchers in terms of the notion of Design.

Design, as I discussed in the introduction, is both a structure constituting a set of resources and the process of creating resources for meaning making. In the case of language, which is the best-known modality, these resources include grammar, words, pragmatics, and information structure, among others (New London Group 1996/2000, p. 27).[4] However, Design pervades communication, though it takes radically different forms. For example, in dance it involves the elements of choreography and the semiotics of movement. In the spatial modality it may involve architecture or engineering. What Design allows us to do is extend the type of rigorous analyses of complex systems that characterize linguistic investigation into other areas of communication. It offers a linguistic sensibility, and it is no accident that many members of the New London Group, including Gee, Cazden, Fairclough, and Kress, were trained in linguistics.

Specifically, my contribution in this book is to integrate the logical theory of information provided by situation theory into the notion of Design of academic achievement. That Design is proposed to be the structure of The Academic Achievement Game, in the sense that it involves information operated on according to rules. The question posed at the beginning, *How can students be successful in college?* is answered in terms of the rules of this game, their knowledge of those rules, and their skill at employing them to attain high grades. These rules constrain and order the possible movements of information and types of information that can be moved in certain ways. The answer also involves strategies for success employed by students and the results of those strategies. This understanding is made possible only because the students and faculty—who are also players in a way—realize the structure of their ways of playing the game as they play it. In the end, there are really only two questions in this study:

- What does the Design of academic literacy look like for the four student participants?
- How do their differences in Design affect their academic achievement?

NOTES

1. This assertion conveniently ignores the fact that testing, particularly the more conservative forms of it, is found worldwide.

2. For those interested in how it is possible to measure reduction of uncertainty, it works as follows: The information has a value of four bits because before the call, the certainty can be considered to be 1 in 64 and after it, 1 in 4. Now, $64 = 2^6$ and $4 = 2^2$, and subtracting the exponents 2 from 6 yields 4. Later, after the interviews, if he is chosen as the successful candidate, his uncertainty reduces to 1. This can be understood as a reduction of two bits since the reduction from 4 to 1 constitutes one from 2^2 to 2^0. Quantities that are not powers of two have fractional exponents.

3. In fact, that confidence has been quantified in item response theory (see, e.g., Hambleton 1989).

4. Page indications refer to the 2000 version.

Chapter 3

Methods

Because qualitative multicase studies have proven so fruitful in exploring many aspects of academic literacy, the same method was chosen for this research. This study, like any qualitative research, was designed to explore processes rather than support or refute hypotheses. There are no claims for generalization; findings should be considered as starting points for either hypothesis confirmation through quantitative methods or further refinement in other qualitative studies (e.g., Merriam 1988; Hammer 1994; Bogdan and Biklen 1998). I should note an exception to this modesty. I have already asserted that the game itself is probably universal. Although this idea arose from my observation of what these students were doing, the claim for universality does not depend on these data. It is supported by the analysis of the literature as described in the previous chapter. The data here only show how the students in this study play the game.

In spite of the precedents of other qualitative case studies, it might be claimed that the gaining of these kinds of insights into another's experience would be better served by a full ethnographic treatment, including participant observation such as that of Moffatt (1991). This anthropologist lived part-time with the Rutgers undergraduates he studied. The description using such an approach would undoubtedly be thicker and would provide more triangulation because behavior can be examined exhaustively in this setting. Correspondingly, there would be less reliance on interviewees' possibly self-serving comments. Nevertheless, academics constitute only a portion of an undergraduate's life, and in fact, Moffatt has far more to say about the social aspects of life at Rutgers than he does about the academic ones. Furthermore, studying takes place often between mind and page, and so the intervention of an observer would likely distort the entire process, if the observer could access it at all. Ultimately, this approach just provides too wide a lens for an examination of academic literacy.

By the same token, it might be thought that one could gain a better understanding of what students do with course content by a more direct attack, such as think-aloud protocols. This would provide data in real time and so eliminate the problems associated with students' perception changing between time of actual studying and that of interview. However, such work has proven most valuable in providing close-up views of specific academic processes such as reading (e.g., Block 1986) or writing (Flower 1989). It is true that both these authors speculate on the role of tasks in determining their result, but they cannot actually show how different tasks change students' approaches; that was not the purpose of their research. To do so requires an examination of a range of tasks in a naturalistic context, which only a qualitative case-study approach supplies (see also Merriam 1988). Here the lens is too narrow and, again, the danger of an effect of intervention is also great.

Therefore, while I acknowledge the limits of the method, I think that it is the best one available for this kind of research, and those advantages are the reason that it has proven so popular and insightful in other academic literacy studies.

PARTICIPANTS

For reasons of practicality, I decided to collect data from a small number of participants during the natural academic period at MSU, one eleven-week quarter. Participants were recruited through a variety of means designed to maximize the pool of potential students. These included posted announcements, class visits the previous quarter, and even chance encounters prior to the beginning of classes of the autumn quarter 1994. Participants were selected from among the twenty-four volunteers to balance difference and similarity in a number of personal and academic characteristics. The reason for this balance was that I wanted data that would hint at the causes of different outcomes in a variety of different circumstances, including different courses, grades, types of assessments and tasks, and so on. However, I also wanted to achieve enough coherence to allow comparability between respondents, and this requires that they share certain qualities. Therefore, I decided to narrow the study down to four undergraduates of similar ethnocultural background who shared a single social science major but who would differ in terms of gender, levels of achievement, and years of study. I chose the social sciences because of the variety of literacy tasks—from essayistic interpretation to quantitative analysis—that characterizes the component fields. Nevertheless, when I was unable to find four undergraduate volunteers with those qualities within a single major, I expanded the scope to include any social science major. The multiplicity of majors was less a distortion than one might initially expect because of the wide variety of classes these students took.[1] One student, in fact, because of her work requirements ended up taking no major classes the study quarter, and another took only one. These respondents, identified by pseudonym along with some general data about them, are listed in Table 3.1. The classes were not the official catalog titles (which might compromise instructors' anonymity) but the terms used by the respondents to refer to the classes.

Table 3.1
Student Participants in the Study

Student	Year	GPA[a]	Major	Classes
Greg	5th	3.85	Sociology-German	Sociology Statistics, Changing Family, Sociology Methods, Modern European History
Carmin	3rd	3.46	Social Work	Human Development, Introduction to Theater, Quantitative Methods Social Work Policy
Sophie	3rd	2.85	Social Work	Introduction to Chemistry, Introduction to Political Science
Will	2nd	2.7	Psychology	Psychology Writing Human Biology International Relations

[a]The maximum grade point was 4. This number corresponds to an "A" at MSU, where an A+ is not given. A "B" is equivalent to a 3, a "C" to a 2, a "D" to a 1, and an "F" to a 0.

DATA COLLECTION

The major portion of the data collection consisted of open-ended interviews that took place mostly in my office. A research assistant (Jerome Mescher) and I met with subjects for approximately one hour per week during the quarter and for one follow-up session in the middle of the next quarter. All respondents except Sophie were assiduous in their attendance; she missed three sessions. Interviews were audiotaped, transcribed, and read before the following session to develop lines of inquiry for that session and to think of documents to request from respondents. Questions ranged from entirely open (e.g., "Tell us what you were studying this week?") to requests for close descriptions of test items (e.g., "Why did you choose *D*?"). We also examined responses to these items (e.g., "Were you confident [about your answer]?"), writing assignments (e.g., "How many drafts did you write?"), and readings (e.g., "Was this easy to understand?"). Interview questions on test items and student writing focused on retrospective explanations of reasoning behind choices and beliefs as to where difficulties lay. Frequently, students had the returned test or essay in front of them during the discussion. Responses were not taken at face value, but students were asked to redo tasks, and other efforts at triangulation (e.g., asking faculty about the same items) were employed.

Questions on studying, including reading, and classes were based on logs students kept (e.g., "But you have forty pages [in your log], you skim them?"). Interviews also examined beliefs about the course contents (e.g., "Was this boring?"), anticipation of assessments (e.g., "Will this be easy?"), and methods and strategies used to meet expectations (e.g., "Did you outline?"). As in Hammer's (1994) study, the interviews became more structured and narrowly focused toward the end of the quarter. They dealt less with philosophy and approaches and more with the tasks at hand, a change that reflects not only our increased familiarity with the issues, but also the greater urgency of assessments as the quarter neared its end.

In the last session, early in the following quarter, students were given a sketch of the emerging categories of information and asked for comment. All except for Greg, who did not express interest in advice, were also given suggestions for improving their studying and our analysis of their particular performance. Apart from the act of interviews and the requests to keep logs, no other attempts were made to intervene in students' studying processes apart from one case that will be discussed in Chapter 6.

In addition to students, a total of five faculty were also interviewed. They are listed here with pseudonyms:

- Will's Psychology Writing teaching assistant (TA), Mr. Hill
- Will's Political Science professor, Dr. Haus
- Greg's Sociology Statistics professor, Dr. Tomko
- Carmin's Theatre professor, Dr. Riordan
- One of Sophie's (two) Chemistry professors, Dr. Thomas

Faculty were interviewed only once in their own offices, and faculty interviews were less open-ended than the student interviews were. They examined a range of issues including epistemics, course goals, perceptions of students' abilities, and rationales for grading. More faculty interviews would have been desirable, but a surprising number declined to be interviewed, while others were not interviewed at students' request. In the case of Greg's History professor, an interview was postponed until after the quarter because he was worried about repercussions due to his dislike of this teacher. However, the professor had left the area before the beginning of the next quarter, and so no interview was possible. Questions to instructors varied depending on the student's interactions. All the teachers were told which student was involved in the study, although three (Will's International Relations professor, Carmin's Theatre professor, and Sophie's Chemistry professor) were unable to identify the individuals due the size of their classes. In these cases, questions focused on rationales behind assessments and other assignments and beliefs about grades and learning. In cases where the students were familiar to faculty, there were additional questions concerning the participant's progress and the faculty member's interpretations of some of their actions.

Other data were collected through documents, including those produced by students (i.e., all writings, returned tests, lecture notes, exercises) and faculty (i.e., syllabi, comments on student work), and many assigned readings. Also, students were asked to keep logs of readings and studying done, and all but Greg did so and handed them in regularly. These logs were used to focus interview questions and as data in their own right. All documents were analyzed to triangulate student and faculty perceptions and to better understand task demands.

DATA ANALYSIS

Initial data analysis began early in data collection, and this work provoked the shift in the research focus discussed in the introduction. With this change, the notion of information flow pattern was determined according to which efforts at achievement consisted of a recycling of information from a source, such as texts and lectures, to targets, such as exams or papers. This pattern was then broken down into what became four basic processes, called *operations*, that students perform on information to foment and direct its flow. The term *operation* reflects the active intervention of the student as a player who acts on information. It is an atomic unit, as opposed to a strategy (e.g., Weinstein and Meyer 1986; Nolen 1988), which may consist of a series of operations designed to meet a certain end, such as memorization. The idea is to account for each effort a student makes in advancing content through the system and then to classify these steps into categories depending on what the interaction consisted of. The (admittedly ambitious) goal of this analysis is to develop a formalism—or better allow a formalism to emerge—that can account for the Design of academic achievement. Operations have a fundamental role to play in that Design because they are the basic unit, analogous to moves in the game.

Operations were divided into what eventually came to be called *exposure, extraction, manipulation*, and *display*. This pattern was inducted from students' descriptions of their interactions with course material while studying and fulfilling assessment tasks. Although it evolved considerably during data analysis, the original basic structure forms the foundation of the operations discussed in Chapter 7. After the study quarter, transcripts and logs were read and reread to isolate and extract references to operations. References were categorized by similarities and differences, particularly how well they fit into the four classes. This was done by cutting discussion of references to operations and surrounding contexts out of transcripts and pasting them into operation-specific MS Word documents. At times two or more operations were referred to in tandem (e.g., when a student would discuss reading and highlighting or outlining and reviewing together), and these excerpts were placed into multiple documents. Then each of these documents was reviewed, and each specific mention of the operation was highlighted electronically to isolate it from its context. Transcripts were then reread, and references to operations that did not seem to fit the definition of the category led to questioning and modification of the category and resulting changes to the collections of excerpts. The goal was to find categories of operations that were exhaustive and internally consistent in how they treated information.

An example of a change will serve to illustrate both the process and the nature of the categories. An original category called *finding* was meant to capture what students were doing as they initially read or heard content. However, the original intuition that students read or listened to in class the first time to find information simply proved unsustainable as data analysis proceeded. The students just did not always do so when first reading or attending class. Furthermore, they often repeated reading or reviewed previously extracted material; in both cases they were making themselves aware of information, exposing themselves to it. In either case, these efforts could be accompanied by attempts to find, isolate, and prioritize relevant information, but these were essentially separate activities. Also, an initial reading or lecture could leave them mystified as to the point. In that case, they would have to either discard the possibility of knowing what was meant or go to some effort to recover the meaning, usually by asking a professor or classmate, (re)reading, or just thinking about it. So the category of *finding* was abandoned. Students' first readings or listenings were distributed among *exposure* to describe the placing of content into awareness, *extraction* to describe the informational triage, and *manipulation* to describe their efforts to discern information.

Similarly, when respondents wrote what they knew on an exam and when they did it as part of a study activity in a chapter learning check, they were doing the same thing with the content. Perhaps when they were lucky, even the questions they were responding to were the same. Both cases were considered to be *display* since they were manifestations for inspection of their knowledge. The difference was whether the display was an end game, designed for a teacher to inspect, that is for a grade, or for practice or self-check. Again, the circumstances varied, but the actions of the student remained the same.

In exactly the same way, a taxonomy of six *information types* that students appeared to discriminate began to emerge. The original rough system evolved into *facts, connections, concepts, procedures, principles, and metainformation,* as will be discussed in Chapter 6. However, evidence for an information type was somewhat different from evidence for an operation because students individuated some types. For example, all four students talked about facts and concepts by name. Greg also discussed connections, principles, and procedures, although he used his own terms.

By starting with the explicit references students made to these types, it was possible to begin a preliminary categorization. Examination of students' behavior with regard to various informational demands made it possible to discern a pattern of similarities and differences across the different types. This heuristic began with the types of information that respondents individuated and moved on to those they merely discriminated. What mattered was identifying each type and treating it in a distinctive fashion. For example, they tried to memorize facts, to build connective networks (when they recognized their existence) and to use and/or describe concepts as complex pieces of information. This was true regardless of whether they explicitly recognized the existence of the type by using a word such as "fact" or "concept" to describe it. Finally, by comparing different students' responses to the same types of information, it became possible to see the role the ability to discriminate or individuate different pieces of information has on performance.

Just as with operations, intensive data analysis brought about changes to the information types. Here too data were reexamined, and inconsistencies and vagueness led to questioning of the emerging categories. Overlap was eliminated whenever possible, and mentions of information or of interactions that did not fit into any category were reexamined to see if category definitions needed altering. For example, at first one category was labeled "linguistic information." This consisted of information about generic conventions. In other words, presence or absence of desired rhetorical organization, nonbiased expressions, correct use of jargon, and standard English usage provide information about the writer's competence in specific written genres. However, this category was later broadened beyond language to include all forms of appropriate information displays, including formulas, diagrams, figures, and so on. This change took place after it became apparent that students gained or lost points for their use of these modalities of information presentation in nonlinguistic forms exactly as they did for written language; the students and faculty treated them in much the same way. The broadened category was renamed *metainformation* because it concerned information about information. Similar though less drastic evolutions took place with the other categories. Just as with operations, the references to information types were isolated in separate Word documents and then highlighted and revised.

Reliability of category assignment was checked by having assignment of a small sample of examples (24 out of 557, or 4.3%) duplicated by two checkers. The extracted examples were evenly

Table 3.2
Agreement between Researchers on Categorization of Operations (percentages)

	Percentage of Agreement
MN-Checker 1	83.3
MN-Checker 2	87.5
Checker 1-Checker 2	87.5

distributed among the four participants but otherwise randomly selected. The reliability was more than satisfactory. Table 3.2 shows the percentage of interresearcher agreement.

NOTE

1. It is typical in the United States, unlike in Europe, Asia, and most of Latin America, for students to take most of their classes outside their concentated area of study, their major. This is achieved through so-called "general education" or "distribution" requirements that specify a range of classes outside the area of study, so that everyone takes some math or science, some humanities, and some social science. It is also accomplished through electives, which allow students to select courses of interest in any area.

Chapter 4

The Worth of a Quarter

In the kind of abstract analysis done in this study, it is easy to forget that the study participants are four unique human beings. First of all, these students were studying for various reasons, and these motives were products of what had taken place earlier in their lives and what they imagined would take place afterwards. Even as they attended MSU they had lives, experiences, and goals outside the academic achievement game they played, and those factors influenced the way they played the game. Therefore, although I analyze their responses in terms of informational structures and operations, it is important to remember that these actions and artifacts were created by complex people engaged in a lot more than studying. A virtue of the qualitative case-study methodology is that it allows the analyst and the reader to contextualize the abstract in this more concrete social reality. To help do so, I will outline in narrative form the experiences of these four participants as I saw them.

GREG

I met Greg in a long line at the post office just before the beginning of the quarter. We began to talk, and he joined me in my complaints about the slowness of the service. I then asked him about his studies, and upon hearing that he was a sociology major, I asked him whether he might be interested in the project to take place during the upcoming quarter. He responded enthusiastically. That interest plus his 3.85 GPA, the highest of anyone who had signed up, led me to ask him to participate.

It turned out that Greg had more than just postal inefficiencies to complain about with me. In his fifth year, he had a serious case of "senioritis," a combination of disillusion with college and anticipation and fear of graduation. At first I worried that I was being placed into the role of an academic psychotherapist, and sometimes not only academic because Greg also had issues with his parents that would occasionally come up.

He was the son of two professionals who had high expectations for his success, and he had dutifully fulfilled these expectations in high school and college, which he entered as an honors student. He was in his fifth year, however, because he had begun as an engineering major, and, although he had won some awards in that program, had transferred to the liberal arts, where he co-majored in Sociology and German. Engineering was just too dry for him, too narrowly focused on practical applications. He wanted to learn about the world, and he was thus in sync with the liberal arts philosophy. His German major was complete because he had spent a year abroad in Germany, and he had only several sociology classes and general education requirements to finish. His classes are shown again in Table 4.1, together with the departments they were housed in.

Greg was every bit as brilliant academically as his GPA would indicate. In addition, he saw himself as an intellectual as a subcultural identification. He played in a jazz band and had little interest in popular culture, be it television, music, or movies. He was concerned with politics and held leftist opinions; on the other hand, he was an active member of a quite traditional Christian denomination. He was also highly idealistic, and it appeared that MSU was falling way short of his expectations, particularly regarding how the grading process interfered with the university's promise of learning. His first three interviews document his plans to escape the trap of grading, as well as his doubts about whether he would actually be able to continue with this independent trajectory once the

Table 4.1
Greg's Classes

Course	Department
Changing Family	Sociology
Statistics	Sociology
Research Methods	Sociology
Modern European History	History

Cs began to role in. All these issues come together in the following description of what happened when he first made a decision to take grades less seriously just before leaving for Germany:

Greg: I know darn well the worth of a quarter during the quarter and when I finish it; so I got the report card and I, I didn't open it. I mean it was meaningless to me. And I was going through this action of not looking at it because I said if I look at it, what's that gonna do? Am I gonna go back to tempting myself with this, this mentality that I'm trying to reject, or I'm trying to overcome by looking at it? And so I told my mom when she asked me, "You didn't open your report card?" I said, "Yeah I don't care." And it hurt her feelings, and I should have watched what I said because to my parents, those grades are a symbol of putting their son through college, and if they can't separate it right now, I have to respect that. They can't separate the grades from the knowledge. And family relations are important to me enough that I know that I'm really gonna try to do things as much as I can not to stress them, even if it means not telling them . . . what might happen to grades.

The motivations for the change in his "system," as he described it, was that he saw little practical return for the efforts he had been making in getting grades:

Greg: I realized that I had taken thousands of notes in college and high school, and paid attention in class, and when I look back and see what I actually remember from it, it's very, very little, so I question, "OK, why put all that effort in? Is it useful? Is it important? Is it practical?"

His efforts to carry out this rebellion took several forms that would not please many teachers. For example, he believed that his statistics class repeated a lot of the material he had covered in his junior year, so he sold his statistics textbook soon after buying it and instead took a previous edition out of the library. He also began to attend class and recitation irregularly. This created an ethical conundrum for him, however. He imagined that his teacher, noticing his lack of engagement, might take it personally, and he decided to tell her his reasons so that she would understand that his behavior was not aimed at her personally. So he went to her office and explained all this to a mildly surprised Professor Tomko. He even discussed his lack of interest in grades and his beliefs about the importance of learning with her in her office. She was, as all college professors are, familiar with apathetic students, but not those who justify their anomie to her in detail. He also soon stopped attending his Modern European History survey because he believed the instructor was acting like a bad high school teacher. Although he never stopped attending the Changing Family seminar, he did his readings irregularly; however, he did express regret for his inability to get to them. Instead, he began to audit an introduction to Modern Greek class that interested him but was irrelevant to his graduation requirements. Only Methods was not a source of conflict for him.

As time went on, the tensions provoked by this rebellion became too much for him, as he had suspected they would. He actually failed a Statistics test, which told him that "something was not learned," and got poor grades on some exercises. Fortunately for his GPA and for this study, by the fifth week of the quarter he was applying himself fully in all his classes except History, but he really did not need to make much effort in this class. He began to read more of the material in that class to compensate for his lack of attendance, and he did return to lectures in the final weeks of the quarter. He also returned to his Statistics class and began to read more consistently for Changing Family.

In the end, he managed to get an A– in History, a B+ in Changing Family, a B+ in Methods, and a C+ in Statistics. This was the first C grade of his life and his worst overall academic quarter. He went on to study for a master of arts degree in social work and, interestingly enough, became an undergraduate advisor while doing so. He looked back on the quarter as a difficult one for him personally. He has long had an interest in doing doctoral studies, and may pursue this interest in the future. He is the only respondent I remain in contact with.

CARMIN

Carmin signed up for the study during the previous spring quarter in a sociology class whose TA allowed me to recruit. She was from a socioeconomic environment very different from the one Greg was from—perhaps one of the macrosocial categories most neglected by educational research—the European-American rural working class. Her mother was a high school dropout and her father a high school graduate with no college education. She also had family members in the Amish community through a grandfather who had left that religion. Education was not a priority in her family, and her parents made no effort to help her or her siblings in their studies at any point, although she was careful to note that they did not discourage her either. Carmin reported their attitude was, "If that's what you want to do."

Still, she had been picked out early on in elementary school as college material and was placed in academic tracks throughout her school career. She arrived at MSU, therefore, with a preparation comparable to that of middle-class students, but with a working-class striver practicality and a genuine but realistic appreciation for the academy's offerings and limitations. She certainly did not engage in any of Greg's philosophical ruminations; for her, the worth of a quarter was learning and grades together. Not that she confused the two. She said, "Even if it's not interesting, I'm always gonna look for the A in the class," but when a class was interesting, "I would spend more time actually knowing it not trying to get the A. The A might not even be as important to me."

During the study, Carmin was in her first junior quarter, which she entered with a 3.46 GPA. This was the first quarter focused on her recently declared social work major. Three of her four classes were in this major (Table 4.2).

Her decision to enter this field was motivated by a combination of what she felt were attractive career possibilities and the fact that she enjoyed a psychology class she had taken previously. More negatively, it was also in part a compromise due to a mistaken perception of her limitations. These resulted from what could only be considered educational malpractice, in particular the misuse of psychometric instruments in high school:

Carmin: They had those tests that they tell you what you're best suited for. [The high school guidance counselor] told me to stay away from sciences, and so ever since then I've had the biggest fear of science, and I took chemistry and biology in college, and I got B+ and A–, and I've come to the realization that I can do science.

The evident result of this misdiagnosis: one less potential female science major.

Still, she began her major with a good deal of enthusiasm. She enjoyed challenges and felt excited about moving on to her major as a first step into her future career. Sadly, this enthusiasm lasted

Table 4.2
Carmin's Classes

Course	Department
Policy	Social Work
Quantitative Methods	Social Work
Human Development	Social Work
Introduction to Theatre	Theatre

only two weeks, and she began to feel that the classes were too easy. By the fourth week, she dismissed the social work major in the following terms:

Carmin: A lot of it seems to be common knowledge, and they throw a theory in to explain it. And how I see it, my little sister could go through and read that stuff and given enough time, she would know it. There's no in-depth thought that would go into it from what I see.

As a result, she felt that she was not being "challenged at all," which led to such frustration that she began to disengage from the reading. She just did not need to do it. More remarkably, she began to rethink her whole career plan and decided to go into occupational therapy, one of the majors she had originally considered but discarded because of the heavy science requirements. Still, she was reluctant to criticize her teachers, instead blaming a mismatch between herself and social work as a discipline:

Carmin: I think that's what social work means. I don't think there's anything wrong with the program. I just don't think the program's right for me because I don't feel that it's stimulating my thought in any way, but a lot of people in my class would think that it's interesting, and they are challenged, but to me I'm not finding that.

In the end, she changed her major, although that required a transfer to a different university. As the quarter went on, she began to make less and less effort because she felt she did not need to work. She could not understand how her classmates could spend so much time studying that material, and she understood even less how they could come to the conclusion that it was difficult. In the end, she got A's in all her social work classes.

The only academic miscalculation she made involved her Introduction to Theatre class. As I mentioned in the introduction, in this class she decided to only buy the plays, avoiding the expensive theoretical textbook. She did this despite the fact that the instructor had warned students that some information on exams would come from this book and would not be mentioned in class. Carmin's decision not to buy the book was largely based on three factors. First, Theatre seemed an inherently easy subject. Second, the class was an introductory level. Third, some friends who had previously taken the class and had gotten A's had told her the book was actually unnecessary because all the exam questions based on material not covered in class had "obvious" answers. She decided she would be better off protecting her budget and using her time elsewhere. In fact, she needed the book and ended up with a disappointing C+.

SOPHIE

Sophie was also a junior social work major who signed up for this study through a class. However, these were about the only ways she resembled Carmin. Although she came from a middle-class professional family—her mother recently completed graduate studies, and her father had a B.A.—she was given little support for her education at MSU. In fact, she said that her parents had told her that barring emergencies, she would have to pay her own way in both her living expenses and tuition because the family had already spent their higher education budget on her brother. Nevertheless, because of her parents' relatively high income, she was ineligible for much need-based financial aid. She appeared more stoic than resentful about this lack of family assistance; her anger was directed at the financial aid regulations that would not consider in their calculations the fact that she was getting no support. She only admitted, when asked directly, the unfair and possibly sexist character of her family's decisions that had left her in this strapped condition. She expressed no overt recriminations toward them.

The lack of assistance did cause her, unfortunately, to drop all but two classes the first week of the study quarter because she needed time to work and to avoid the expense of taking more classes. Both remaining classes were general education requirements (Table 4.3).

My fear of not finding replacements at this late date combined with Sophie's strong interest in participating in the study prevented me from dropping her when I found out about her decision. In the end, although she was the least reliable respondent in terms of attendance, she offered a number of interesting insights into study processes, particularly those that, I suspect, characterize underachievement, although she was at no point in danger of failing.

She was interested in neither Chemistry nor Political Science, but she made sure she passed them. Although she always hoped for a higher grade, it was never much more than a wish because she engaged in what might be called a minimum-sufficient-effort strategy. She attended class regularly and completed more of her

Table 4.3
Sophie's Classes

Course	Department
Introduction to Chemistry	Chemistry
Introduction to Political Science	Political Science

readings than Greg or Carmin did, but she did them at times in front of the television. In large part, Sophie blamed the MSU system for her lack of interest. Among other things, she claimed the university was hypocritical. For example, the Political Science professor promised a broadening of students' perspectives on his syllabus. He told them specifically that they would understand the nightly news better. However, Sophie believed he did not provide any such insights. Looking over the syllabus, we had this discussion:

Investig.: What do you think that you're supposed to get out of college?
Sophie: [laughs] An education.
Investig.: How do you understand an education?
Sophie: You become more aware of what's going on around me, throughout the world and in my immediate area.
Investig.: So substantially you agree with what he's saying [on the syllabus]?
Sophie: Yeah sure.
Investig.: You just don't think . . .
Sophie: He's not doing what he's saying. It seems to me.

She therefore conceived of both of her classes as hoops to jump through and looked forward to classes that were directly related to social work after she arrived at the other side. Furthermore, she recalled having taken psychology and sociology classes and having applied herself thoroughly to them. She said she would do so in the future as the classes related more to her interests and professional needs. However, for this quarter, studying was just one part of Sophie's life rather than the center of it. She wanted to do a good job, but neither that desire nor the material itself motivated her enough to make the kind of effort to get an A or even a B. She received two Cs.

WILL

Minnesota radio raconteur Garrison Keillor once told a joke to illustrate a supposed Midwestern cultural norm of always putting on the best face in any situation. Keillor imagines a group of Midwesterners talking about the sinking of the Titanic in which one concludes, "Well, it was a good trip until that point. . . ." The others then all echo this sunny outlook.

Although the other students—through their complaints and rebellions—did not support this stereotype, Will had an unfailing ability to respond with maximum optimism to his collisions with academic icebergs. Although he never failed a class, he did consistently sink beneath his own hopes and expectations. Yet he always expressed the belief that he was "going up" in GPA. He consistently believed he would "do better on the next test." Difficulties were almost always a "challenge." Only once, after five poor grades on papers in his psychology writing class, did he finally admit to frustration and anger. Yet even here he was unable to blame the teacher—who he liked—but put the onus on himself. He felt he should not get credit for what he should have learned in high school.

I met Will though a chance encounter. He was changing lightbulbs in a campus building in his capacity as a work-study student, and I began a conversation with him. When I found that he fit the profile, I asked him to sign up. He did so enthusiastically. I suspect now that he did so in good part because he imagined he would gain some insights that would help him succeed. If so, he was probably right, although that was not the purpose of the study, a point I made clear to him right from the beginning.

Will was an upper sophomore the quarter of the study, and he had a 2.7 GPA. He was of urban working-class origin from a small industrial city an hour away from MSU, and, like Carmin, he was the first in his family to go to college. However, unlike her, he had been an undistinguished high school student, who, as he told it, woke up one day before graduation with the realization that his comfortable teenage life of going from his room at home to school to visits with friends was inevitably coming to an end. Encouraged by his parents, he decided to go to community college, where he placed into a remedial reading class. He found this fact so embarrassing that he only admitted it more than half way into the quarter and only after much probing of his community college background. Upon graduation from this two-year school, Will transferred to MSU, though only as a sophomore.[1] This was his moment of triumph; he recalled himself thinking "I'm at MSU!"

Yet like a number of community-college transfers I have worked with over the years in my own classes, he soon felt out of his depth. His worries about his lack of preparation did not impede the size of his dreams, however. He was a psychology major who was enthusiastic about the material, more so than any of the other participants were of their studies. He even intended to go to graduate school and become a clinical psychologist. Nonetheless, he was taking only one psychology class as he was finishing his general education requirements, and had reduced his load to three to give himself more study time for each and so boost his GPA (Table 4.4).

To arm himself for success, he bought just about every book on study skills available in the local bookstores, and he even purchased—at considerable expense—a video on academic success. Will

Table 4.4
Will's Classes

Course	Department
Writing	Psychology
International Relations	Political Science
Human Biology	Biology

described this video as mixing inspirational messages with what seemed to be dubious advice based largely on supposed mnemonic tricks. He had already discarded most of the advice as not helpful, but he had not given up the search for a magic bullet. The quarter of the study, for example, he had become an enthusiastic proponent of good time management, and had purchased a series of "Franklin Quest" agendas that organized, supposedly, a person's life in the most efficient manner possible. In fact, time was an issue for him. No other respondent spent anywhere close to the amount of time on their classes as Will: between six to eight hours per day at the books.

However, he did not do well, particularly in biology and psychology. As test after test and paper after paper came back with disappointing C's, Will continued to think that he would finally discover what he needed to do differently to succeed, and he tried one prescription after another. By the middle of the quarter he was recording and transcribing his lectures in biology and psychology, which he would then pore over. Will also had problems unrelated to school that impacted on his ability to function. At the time of the study, he had just been diagnosed with asthma and ended up missing a couple of classes because of doctor's appointments and one class because he was having an attack. He believed that having asthma also affected his performance.

The only exception to this generally dismal picture was his International Relations class. There are good reasons why this class was easier for Will, and I discuss them in the results section. However, it is enough to mention here that he got a full forty out of forty points on the essay portion of his midterm. This result, although it did not correspond to his success on the multiple-choice portion, provided needed outside confirmation for his optimism and support for his self-esteem. Finally, almost at the end of the quarter, he improved in his all-important Psychology Writing class, getting twenty-six out of thirty on the last assignment. He received a B– in that class, a B in International Relations, and a C+ in Biology.

At a follow-up meeting and once more informally when he stopped by to chat the next year, Will reported that he was doing much better, although he had to give up his career plans in psychology. He had gotten so far behind with his GPA that there was little chance of his getting into graduate school, and the whole issue was just creating too much anxiety. He therefore transferred to a business major, where he achieved an A– average while doing a lot less work. It was gratifying for me to hear that he believed that the interview sessions and the follow-up debriefing had the effect of helping him realize where he was wasting effort. He actually laughed about all those hours spent trying to learn material with so little to show for them.

NOTE

1. Community colleges, sometimes called junior or two-year colleges, are U.S. institutions of higher education with the dual mission of preparing students typically not admitted to four-year schools for transfer after two years and others for semivocational or vocational careers.

PART II

CLASSES

Wittgenstein (1953) advises readers of his *Investigations* as they make their way through his work to imagine themselves crisscrossing a conceptual landscape the way that a traveler gets to know a new city. By first taking one route around and then another and then another, both types of explorers come to see not only new places, but also old ones from different directions. After a number of trips, they come to know the territory. McGinley and Tierney take this metaphor as valid for any conceptual learning. Learners only really know a subject after having traversed its conceptual landscape various times from various directions.

In the following four chapters, I will lead readers along four different routes through the same landscape of the academic achievement game, as played by Greg, Carmin, Sophie, and Will during the study quarter. You will see some of the same places from different angles and will visit others only once. At times I, the driver, will stop to explore the locales in detail before moving on. Sometimes when the stop promises to get a bit too tedious but the visit is not yet complete, I will move on with the idea of stopping again on a later trip through. Of course, I could have made different decisions regarding these stops; some of these locales could have been visited in more depth on another trajectory. Be that as it may, I hope that by the end, readers will have a reasonable grasp of the landscape of academic achievement as realized by the participants.

The first trip through, Chapter 5, is appropriately the most superficial because it is designed to get the quickest sense of the lay of the land, or better, the game board. It consists of an exploration of academic achievement as a game-like system. It also depicts the consequences on performance of whether students viewed it that way or not.

Chapter 6 shows the ways the students in the study conceptual-
ized the six different types of content they encountered. It also shows
how the students varied in their grasp of these types of information and the ways these different perspectives on content explain
the different approaches they took to the material.

Chapter 7 travels through the activities the students performed
on this content, dividing it into four different *operations*. Each operation is designed, I argue, to move information from source to
target. Again, the students varied in how much they depended on
each operation, how they ordered them, and what they thought the
effects of each would be. As in the previous cases, these understandings had effects on their performance.

Chapter 8 sums up the sights seen on the previous trip by pre-
senting the game chronologically in three stages. It also explores
some additional areas that were neglected on the earlier journeys
because they do not directly relate to operations or information types
but are still of interest.

Chapter 5

Awareness of Achievement
versus Learning

In Chapter 2, I differentiated the achievement game from learning in terms of the difference found by Entwistle (1987) between two forms of student engagement, the "strategic approach" on the one hand, and "deep" and "surface approaches" on the other. I claimed that this distinction corresponded to different information-flow patterns. In the pattern corresponding to the strategic approach, the flow consists of a recycling of information from curriculum to student and then back to the assessor, the goal of which was to get a grade. I described this pattern as constituting the macrodesign of the academic achievement game. In the case of both deep and surface approaches, there was a one-way flow from curriculum to student, and I described this pattern in terms of learning.

Furthermore, following Pintrich and Garcia (1991), I argued that the distinction between the achievement game and learning was not necessarily an either/or orientation a student had, but that the two goals could be pursued simultaneously. Indeed, many successful students examined in case-study research have done precisely that. After all, if the strategic approach is simply an effective way to get grades, and the deep approach is a good way to learn, there is no reason why students could not do both simultaneously.

I also argued that these flow patterns are not applicable to only transmission models of pedagogy. They also describe constructivist pedagogies when information is understood as encompassing informational structures, including procedural knowledge, forms of critical thinking, and adaptation to social conventions, in addition to facts. Under that broad view, any curricular goal can be understood in informational terms. Similarly, the term "flow" can be applied to instances where a student constructs or reconstructs knowledge found in a curriculum in some form, as well as those cases when the student receives it directly. Given those assumptions, the recycling pattern can be seen as descriptive of what happens in every classroom in which there is teaching and assessment.

Note that although this discussion about achievement and learning is based largely on a critical review of the literature rather than on empirical discovery, I did not arrive at this understanding by simply reading the education literature. I say this because I do not want to be accused of having simply confirmed in the students what I had already decided was true on theoretical grounds. In fact, much of my theoretical grounding came only after I had noticed the phenomena I describe here. I began only with the rhetorical and case-study literature, and my knowledge of situation theory was limited to linguistic phenomena (see Newman 1998). It took a number of years of working through the remaining cognitive, situation-theoretic, and eventually the Multiliteracies work to develop the theoretical component described above and to make claims that the patterns found are universal.

The basic finding I can report here is that the two respondents who had a more nuanced conceptualization of the difference were more successful than the two who distinguished it less neatly. Furthermore, the differences between their understandings suggests that their ability to separate learning from achievement clearly and consistently affected their levels of performance. In particular, the two who more clearly separated the achievement game from learning had an easier time in organizing their studying and were more effective in doing so.

On this point, it is important to note that *all* four case-study participants differentiated the achievement game from learning to some extent. What varied is that the two lower achieving students, Will and Sophie, appeared to be considerably less assured about the achievement game than were the more successful ones, Greg and Carmin. They were less certain about the specifics involved and more readily confused aspects of the game with learning.

To begin with the weakest student, Will made it clear that he understood that there was a difference, but he did so in a way that was riddled by contradictions and uncertainty. For example, he championed a focus on learning over one of just getting a grade as he claimed, "I'm here to learn and to take this into the world and help me my entire life, . . . and so I'd rather learn something than just get a good grade." This positive perspective was confirmed by his practice of keeping all his notes and the books that he found interesting after the quarter so he could refer to them again. Also, he valued his learning in various classes, particularly Psychology classes, and referred to it proudly whenever an opportunity came up to employ it. Nevertheless, he sometimes contradicted this learning-centered perspective. He described grades, not learning, as "the bottom line" and said "the knowledge is secondary I guess. You know, tests don't always test what you know." That was why he also felt he could "learn a lot from a class and still get a B or C." Will also contradicted himself further by saying at another time, "I believe in the grading system, I believe that it's pretty accurate." These contradictions appeared randomly throughout the interviews and varied mainly by topic; I could detect no evolution in his attitudes over time. In fact, the last two statements were from the same interview.

For all that, Will was not entirely unaware of some of the contradictions between the various opinions that he held. For instance, he blamed his lack of preparedness for the paradox of how the grading system could be "pretty accurate" on the one hand, and he could still get a low grade in courses in which he had learned so much on the other. He could not be graded on what he should have learned in high school and was only catching up on in college. However, he subtly but crucially misinterpreted the nature of what he described as "knowledge [the professors] can't grade me on" by including "how to write papers, how I should focus more on how I arrange things in a paper and stuff like along those lines." In other words, he saw the nonmechanical norms of academic writing as falling outside the scope of assessment despite the fact that he was in a psychology writing class where these skills were important curricular objectives. It was not even a question of underpreparedness per se; the instructor told the class and us directly that most of the students in this class had trouble mastering these qualities of good academic writing.

Will's trouble viewing rhetorical norms as targets for grading was actually one of a number of misapprehensions he held regarding the types of information that counted on assessments. Another involved concepts. He voiced the assumption several times that he would be primarily graded on facts and writing mechanics. In particular, he described his difficulties in college generally in terms of his inability to absorb sufficient numbers of low-level features, and his goal for studying was largely to improve his memory. His uncertainty and confusion were also manifested when we asked him to explain why grades were given at all. Note that in the following salad of rationales, many individually show considerable insight into aspects of grading, but there is no coherence among them. There is certainly little questioning as to why these qualities matter; nor does it appear that he had ever thought about this issue before:

Will: Well I think it's to see who puts the effort into what. I think it's more about effort than anything else, and I think the people who have learned tricks that have in turn increased their ability, maybe have learned a trick or a style of how to study things more specifically or know how to pick things out. "OK this will probably be on the test; this will probably be on the test," instead of studying it all have a little bit more of an advantage. But you know I think that's what the grading system is for, is to teach people how to do that, to be able to pick out the importance and you know skim over the less important. I think the grading system is basically to test effort and of course knowledge in a subject. I don't know if it's always accurate, I like to believe that it is for the most part accurate, but I don't know if it's always accurate. Let's see, I think uh, that is a pretty tough question. . . . I mean somebody that might be studying ten hours a day for that class could still end up doing poorly just because they have a hard time understanding that class. . . . The grading system has been a part of everyone's life since they've gone to first grade, that's all there is to it.

Sophie, who had a marginally higher GPA than Will, had a similarly tenuous grasp on the achievement game, although she also claimed that there was a difference between it and learning. She expressed the distinction in terms of a dichotomy between "learning," which she defined as long-term retention, and "memorization," which she defined as short-term. Her view, however, was different from Will's in that she distinguished the two functionally rather than in terms of what types of information would or would not count on assessments. Memorization involved content that would never be used after the test, whereas learning was applied to useful information of whatever type, regardless of whether she would be held accountable for it on tests and papers. She thus argued that she learned more in Political Science than Chemistry saying, "I'll use that" in the future, although her grades in both classes were equal.

Digging a little deeper, this utilitarian approach appeared only to mask a less easily defensible reason why some material might be "learned" rather than just "memorized"; the only reason she would use Political Science was because she liked its content better than that of Chemistry. It was more compelling to her. In fact, Sophie had been complaining throughout the quarter about the focus on Mexico in Political Science. Having missed the strategy of employing this country as an example to illustrate a number of political science concepts and theories, she believed that the class simply concerned facts about Mexico. That was why she accused the instructor of violating the promise on the syllabus that the course would help students understand the evening news. As she put it, this assertion was not true because "there really hasn't been that much in the news about Mexico." So when the material switched to postcommunist Europe, which had been in the news that year, she was able to change her opinion. She claimed, "I really liked what we talked about, communism and all that stuff, it helps me understand what all they've gone through over there."

In sum, for Sophie the difference between memorizing and learning was essentially motivational in nature. Neither was explicitly connected to the grading system, although it could be surmised that grades provided the only motivation, and extrinsic motivation at that, to memorize. On that point, Sophie was no better able than Will to explicate what the grading process accomplished. The closest she got to an answer was to say, "Well you have to have certain requirements to meet whatever, certain goals that the university has and stuff like that." She also appeared not to have thought about grades as a system; grading was just a feature of college life imposed as if by an act of God.

Unlike Sophie and Will, Carmin was able to explain a coherent purpose for grades. She explicitly pointed to a gatekeeping function. Grades served, according to Carmin, "to weed out people that they don't think are going to be successful overall in their career choice." She also pointed to rewards for performance: "You get the scholarships from the grades; you get financial aid from the grade; you get the job from the grade." She also understood that the system was seriously flawed because, among other things, "some people don't test well," although she did not "see any way to get around it."

Carmin used language similar to Sophie's in some respects; she also distinguished between "memorization" and "learning," but the meanings that these two students ascribed to the terms appeared to be different. Carmin's understanding was more subtle and insightful. She argued, "I'm almost going to say that grading is more your memorization, not your learning, but there might be circumstances where it is not." For Carmin, "memorization" included largely facts that were spit back, and it was the result of considerable strategizing and planning. "Learning," was, if not effortless, at least not the result of such calculation. They were different processes. In the first interview, before Carmin became disillusioned with her major, she thought that in "a lot of my classes, my social work classes, psychology and sociology, the classes, like, that really interest me, I t..ink that I naturally absorb them easier." In those classes, Carmin said, "I would spend more time actually knowing it not trying to get the A. The A might not even be as important to me." Furthermore, as this quote implies, Carmin assumed that attention to the achievement game might actually detract from learning.

On this point, it is important to note how important achieving was to Carmin. She said repeatedly during the quarter that she was always going for an A in every class, no matter how uninteresting that class was. This ambition followed directly from the rewards she saw flowing from the grading system; she did not want to end up on the wrong side of a selection that might impact on her financial aid or her future career. She was thus very disappointed with herself for not following her own philosophy in this matter in the case of Theatre, where she felt that she had been overconfident as well as misled by other students.

Greg also ascribed a social sorting function to the grading system. When I asked why the system existed, he pointed out that "we like to differentiate people" and that "I think that they are separating people out" by grading them. He went further in his social analysis of the system than Carmin did. He felt that grading reflected larger social norms because "it goes along with a lot of things that we are used to: stratification, competition, judgment, success, progress, bigger-better-faster, smarter. . . . You take this class, how well did you perform?" He was far less interested in the material rewards than was Carmin, perhaps the result of never having had to confront material privation or worry much about financial aid.

His analysis of what goes into grades, how they are determined, was also more detailed than Carmin's. Performance on assessments, he said, was based on various criteria, making much the same point of the inevitability of the recycling Design I have been arguing for earlier:

Greg: [Students are graded] on the ability to reproduce information or often use thought processes creatively. It depends on what kind of class you're in really. I didn't feel like I was required to do anything really creative in the history class; it was kind of recant [*sic*] the formula of whatever. But maybe a writing class would involve style creativity, but still there is a standard that is looked for.

Needless to say, Greg was very critical of the grading system. On his view, the purpose of college should be learning, seen in terms of self-improvement. He expressed a belief that a healthy approach to college for a student would be to ignore grades as much as possible and consider them as only "side effects of the system that you're in." By contrast, an unhealthy one "would be to learn things not to understand them but so that you can spit them out and get a grade ultimately." He criticized himself for taking the unhealthy approach for most of his academic career, and his unhappiness was a major motive for his rebellion against the achievement game.

Importantly, the relative clarity of the students' visions corresponded to the approaches they took to their studying. Greg, like Carmin, knew he needed to plan out how to do well on tests and how to write papers and to perform exercises by working backwards from an assessment instrument to the materials and classes. Greg's plans, however, were more detailed and complex than Carmin's. Greg described the way he used to consider the assessment in studying as follows:

Greg: It's usually not that hard to guess what's gonna be on the exam. You go through the chapters, you pick out the main topics of each chapter, and you don't go into the details. If you only have fifty minutes for an exam, you know that you will probably not be tested over the fourth level step of a process that you only discussed until the third level in class. You know if he talked about sampling methods, then he would be talking about probability and nonprobability and then he would break the probability down into a number of different examples of probability sampling and then he would break down nonprobability sampling.

In terms of action, this approach led to various efficiencies. In general, he treated every exam as a take home test with questions he imagined would appear. He could take this calculation to a high level of finesse. For example, when it came to his history final, Greg managed to find out that the professor's dissertation dealt with the Russian Revolution. He therefore assumed that this question would appear as an essay test question and prepared accordingly. He was right, although he admitted that had he been forced to answer a question on another topic, he might have had considerably more difficulty. He also spent less time on Germany or Poland, both of which interested him more for personal reasons, such as his year abroad and his Polish ancestry.

Carmin's plans also tended to consider the test, but I never observed her actually trying to figure out what would appear in such detail. It is difficult to say, however, whether this reflected a lack of wiliness or simply the ease of her social work courses. Still, she did think out and plan, even to the point of calculating what grade she would need on her Development final to receive an A in the course. She then decided that since this "magic number" was lower than she could imagine getting, she went out the night before the exam for a birthday party. Her calculations in that class turned out to be correct.

It would appear that Greg and Carmin's better sense of the basic structure of the game, what it led to, why it was in place, and how it functioned allowed them more leeway and control in their studying. They anticipated assessments and thought backwards from them as they planned out their studying. They eliminated extraneous information earlier on in the process, thought about teachers' expectations and personalities, and planned how to spend their time and effort. Whereas they strategized, Sophie and Will thrashed about. They acted as if the assessment were just that, a measure of how well they learned the entire content of the curriculum and so set about to do so. Because this was an impossible task, they were frustrated. They used trial and error to see if one study technique might work and then if another one might do the trick better. Neither had a sense of the big picture, and neither acted like they did. In sum, although no participant explicitly explained the achievement game in terms of the recycling Design I have ascribed to it— Greg came the closest—the more successful ones acted as if this were the case. They discriminated the game.

Such results, limited as they are to four students, do not of course come close to *proving* that a clear conceptualization of the difference between grades and learning should lead to more academic success. However, they do suggest that greater appreciation of this difference might make for an improvement because it leads to a clearer understanding of the tasks at hand and less and more ordered improvisation. Therefore, it makes sense to look at the division between the depictions as *suggesting* that a clear differentiation between learning and achievement is likely to be a contributing factor in successful outcomes in college. On this point, it is interesting to note that the sorting function and the competitive aspects ascribed by Greg and Carmin to grading fit perfectly into a game-like view of academic achievement. Furthermore, this hypothesis is strengthened in the next two chapters, which explore two aspects of the Design of the achievement game. In particular, these chapters show how the different degrees of finesse and planning mapped exactly into levels of success.

Chapter 6

Types of Information

By types of information, I am referring to a way of classifying course content in terms of the students' perspectives on its structure and use. Because it depends on perspective, this taxonomy is an illustration of how cognition is situated or distributed in the sense in which cognitive scientists such as Norman and his colleagues (e.g., Rumelhart and Norman 1988; Norman 1990, 1993; Zhang and Norman 1994) use the terms. The situatedness is derived in this case from the fact that students categorize course content simultaneously in terms of what the content itself affords and their own conceptual schemes.

Classifications of content in terms of informational structure are not entirely new in educational research. As discussed briefly in Chapter 2, there is a similar effort in epistemics to describe how students' conceptualizations relate to their learning. To recapitulate the main findings, these studies found that students who hold more interrelated and more dynamic views of the material have better results. By contrast, those students who tend to see course content as independent inert pieces of information seem to have more difficulty. However, some of these studies have added a caveat to this general trend. They have seen these properties not just as products of the student's approaches to content but also as a function of the way the professors organize content and tasks in their classes. This is a point made by Pintrich and Garcia (1991, p. 378): "Rather than two types of learners it is possible to hypothesize that there will be students who have different patterns of goals and use a variety of different cognitive and metacognitive strategies and that their patterns may vary by the academic task or course context." In other words, some content and some tasks or presentations demand different degrees of interrelatedness and different levels of dynamism. How the information is presented by readings, instructors, and tasks also undoubtedly has an impact.

A limitation of these studies is a lack of a system for describing the interrelatedness and dynamism they find in content. Without this kind of organizing paradigm, the descriptions of specific instances of students' constructions appear to be ad hoc, and the conclusions can become speculative. It can also be difficult to compare the findings with those of other studies because it is hard to know whether two authors are referring to the same concept with a single term or two different concepts with the same term. One contribution of my present work is to provide this kind of formalism. This formalism emerged empirically from a close analysis of the ways that respondents interacted with the content of their courses as well as the professors' depiction of their goals and is grounded theoretically by using the semantics developed by situation theorists. My formalism consists of a taxonomy of six categories of information that respondents discriminated.

The notion of discrimination, as opposed to individuation, is important because it allowed me to devise a classification based not only on students' *descriptions* of their understanding of content but also on *how they responded systematically* to it in ways that they might not have been able to explain. The actual categorizations can be divided into two classes, declarative and procedural, and three levels of abstraction (Table 6.1). Those students who were more successful were able *to discriminate information on the more abstract ends of the scale* more consistently.

The contribution made here by applying situation theory is the ability to describe this information in formulaic terms using the notation of the theory, thereby anchoring it in the universality that characterizes mathematical notation. In this way, the different types

Table 6.1
Types of Information

	Declarative	Procedural
Concrete	Fact	Process
│	Connection	Principle
Abstract	Concept	Metainformation

of information can be identified more consistently and systematically than would be possible with simple subjective judgment. If it is not describable in terms of the formula, the information does not belong in that category. Equally important, the formalism reveals characteristics that show how one type of information relates to other types and how these characteristics may also have consequences for how students interact with content. In what follows, I will discuss each of these categories individually, though due to the nature of the data collected, some categories receive a more complete treatment than others.

FACTS

All the respondents in this study—even the weaker ones—mentioned "facts" as a kind of information that they had to interact with, implying that they individuated them as a category. Moreover, they all referred to them, at times, with a physically graphic contempt, speaking of having to "regurgitate" or "spit them back." Will complained that fact-driven courses did not permit him to use his interpretive skills. Greg protested that his European History course was "real heavy on facts and dates" like "a bad high school class." Carmin went so far as to claim that facts were not even learned but memorized. She put her feelings in terms of meaning by saying that "memorizing is just facts, but if those facts don't mean anything to you, then you haven't learned anything." Sophie expressed her early problems in Political Science in terms of a lack of cohesion that was the result of the heavily factual content: "The more and more we get into [it], it's just facts . . . nothing really gets the whole thing together."

In situation theory, the atomic nature of facts, evident in Sophie's remark, can be seen in how they are defined as individual units of information. In the theory, informational units—whether they are true, false, or otherwise—are called *infons*; facts are defined as *true* infons, that is those that—postmodern hackles notwithstanding—accurately depict reality. Infons can be written formulaically as follows:

$$\sigma = <<R, a_1, \ldots a_n>>$$

The σ represents the infon as a whole. R represents a relation—some kind of predication, specification, or modification usually expressed using a verb, adjective, quantifier, or preposition in human languages. The elements indicated by a are arguments, which, following the usage of that term in formal logic, refer to entities or concepts that are being related, including individuals (people or things), times, situations, locations, polarity (yes or no), or other infons. The subscripts *1* through *n* differentiate the arguments from one another and serve here to indicate that the number of such arguments is not fixed. The infon is therefore, as a whole, a statement of relation between arguments, in more traditional terms, a proposition (see also Kruglanski 1989, 1990 for an account of course content in terms of propositions). Take for example, a proposition such as *Bush lost the popular vote in 2000*. Using the formula given, we could say

$$\sigma = <<lose,\ Bush,\ the\ popular\ vote,\ the\ year\ 2000,\ 1>>$$

The relation is lose. The arguments are "Bush"—an *individual*, "the popular vote"—a *situation*, "the year 2000"—a *time*, and "1"— a positive polarity (i.e., that the item of information is an affirmation as opposed to a negation). Losing is the relation Bush has to the popular vote in that election year. It is possible to think of other arguments, including the United States as a location, or to break down the popular vote into other arguments.[1]

Although in this case the formula buys us little, the notation will become useful in the next section when I illustrate how facts hang together. All I want to say here is that defining facts in terms of their parts and distinguishing those parts, as the formula does, makes clear that like people, facts are not islands. Effectively, in the real world, there is no such thing as "just a fact." As a situated concept, facts are facts because they were treated that way, not necessarily because of the intrinsic nature of the factual material. So when facts are linked and considered in relation to one another, they cease to be only facts in the students' minds. The same can be said for cases when facts are used dynamically to interpret other information. By contrast, what might naturally be considered complex, tightly interwoven schemata, such as paradigms or theories, can be considered facts by students when and if they are so treated by the instructor or textbook. So Carmin believed she was being required to memorize facts even when the subject matter consisted of complex psychological theories:

Carmin: A lot of it was Piaget, Ericson, Freud, and have to memorize the ages, stages, the information within the stages.

Investig.: Was this more fact or concepts?

Carmin: More facts.

In other words, although professors may believe they are teaching theories because they are aware of the big picture, students may not agree if that picture is not made clear to them. When the information is presented in simple formats of "yes/no," "this researcher said this," "this theory states that," students may feel they are only learning facts.

Yet all facts are not equal. Students know they need to learn some but not all facts presented to them, and this led respondents to engage in a process of triage (discussed in detail in the next chapter). Typically, they would prioritize in terms of their understanding of the rest of the course content (see also Nist, Simpson, Olejnik, and Mealey 1991; Van Meter, Yokoi, and Pressley 1994; Hynd and Stahl 1998). The comparison implies that they were moving beyond facts because the relations of more or less importance imply a consideration of facts in a connected way. Carmin and Will labeled the unimportant facts "details," and whatever they were called, they were not considered by participants to be fair game for assessment.

Some faculty were aware of this issue. Professor Haus complained that the textbook he was using "quite frankly is more fact driven than I want." He said the philosophy behind the book was to "have chart after chart without explanation, the twelve most important countries on this measure on this or that." The significance of these measures was left implicit, and therefore such a text required that he provide the framework in which the facts could make sense and become useful. If facts were not used as a tool for greater understanding, he believed, they mainly would be accumulated by students, spat back on exams, and forgotten afterward.

Of course, sometimes faculty and students disagree on what is and is not important. A vivid example presented itself in the quiz on *Oedipus Rex* in Carmin's Theatre class. The students had been told there would be no "picky details" on these quizzes. However, the criterion for determining a "picky detail" is problematic, and when the quiz required the identification of the oracle that predicted Oedipus's fate, Carmin protested publicly in front of the whole class. The name of the oracle was not germane to the action or theme, she argued to the TA, though to no avail. Since the purpose of the quiz was to make sure that students read, she had a point, although the TA evidently felt that the answer, Delphi, was sufficiently prominent. Carmin had never heard of this oracle before and did not evaluate the play in light of the big picture of Greek mythology, in which Delphi certainly has a major iconic value. Instead, she saw it only in terms of the internal structure of the play, where it was simply the name of a place where something happened: the very embodiment of a "picky detail."

Since the type of information is the result of the students' perceptions as much as the nature of the material itself, it is interesting to explore factors orienting students toward facts rather than other categories. Some researchers in epistemics (Langer 1992; Haas 1994; Wineburg 1997) have suggested that an important factor is what students anticipate will appear on assessments, a view that is consonant with the macrostructure of academic achievement outlined in the previous chapter. Carmin and Greg associated facts with multiple-choice tests, and each item on these tests does usually form a simple proposition. Moreover, an item is typically unrelated to its neighbors.

Consider the following two examples taken at random from Greg's Methods midterm exam, which is notable because its contents seem to be less about facts and more about principles of good research. Yet these items, which take two characteristic types of structures of multiple-choice tests, can be understood as being answered by the formation of a single proposition. Item (1) is a question plus potential answers, whereas (2) contains an incomplete sentence as a kind of stem followed by choices needed to complete it. In item (1), a proposition is created when the choice *a, b, c,* or *d,* is substituted for the wh-phrase in the question. In item (2), the choice added on to the stem creates the proposition (Hill 1992, 1995, 2000; Hill and Larsen 2000):

(1) Which of the following is NOT a common error made in writing survey questions?

a. a double-barreled question

b. leading respondents

c. coercing respondents to keep answering

d. asking questions to which people keep saying yes

(2) A researcher should always ensure that participants in their research project are

a. free of any risks

b. have minimal risks of any kind

c. fully informed of the exact purpose of the research

d. only at risk of voluntary withdrawal

In the first case, the proposition resulting from the selection of the target is

Coercing respondents to keep answering is not a common error made in writing survey questions.

The second presents a complication. If the target choice *b* is added to the stem, the result would be the following ungrammatical sentence:

*A researcher should always ensure that participants in their re-
search project are have minimal risks of any kind.*[2]
The test writer should have left out the verb *are* from the stem
and added it to choices *a, c,* and *d*.[3] This anomaly was noticed by
Greg, who chose the distractor *c* for this reason, thus fatally over-
estimating the importance of grammaticality to the test writers.[4]
In any case, the point is that each item looked at on its own conveys
a single fact, and indeed most multiple-choice items examined were
of this type. However, the relation between test format and information types is somewhat more complex than it appears by considering only these examples. Greg said that some essay tests could
be largely factual in demand; it depended on what was asked. This
was certainly the case with his History midterm and final exams,
which mainly asked about historical events and personages. Note
the first question from his final:

(3) There were 2 Russian Revolutions in 1917. What exactly happened
and why? What effect did the Russian Revolution have on World War
I and ultimately on the rest of the world?

Greg's successful answer was largely a recitation of events reproduced from course materials.
The third issue regarding facts is their incontrovertibility. Although the notion of truth is notoriously difficult on a philosophical level, within a course truth can be defined in terms of whatever
leads to a correct answer on a test or acceptance in extended writing. This accuracy by fiat is unproblematic for the instructor if it is
accepted by members of the class, but naturally the outside world
can and does intrude. Note the conflict between "classroom truth"
and Greg's own beliefs that led him to argue after class with his
History instructor about denazification in Germany:

Greg: Makes me wonder whether it's really a free marketplace of ideas or
not, but her rationale was: "This is a survey course. I can't talk about
those things. They're too complicated." I said "Well, even if you would
just tell people, 'There's another side to things than what I'm telling
you,' and give them a couple names and say 'if you're interested, go
check it out.'" But I think the danger . . . is that she will make it sound
like that's total fact, and there's no other side to the story.

The certainty of facts may also be a factor in the way students
respond to them affectively. For example, the undergraduates at a
conservative religious university studied by Alexander and Dochy
(1994) and the weaker undergraduates in Hammer's (1994) study
of a physics class at a selective private university showed a prefer-

ence for factual knowledge over deeper, more concept-dependent understandings. It is tempting to speculate that treating course material as facts may require fewer alterations to previous understandings of subject matter and worldview. For this reason, facts can simply be accumulated; it is only when they are actively used (and so cease to be mere facts) that noticing contradictions becomes inevitable, and these incoherencies begin to force a person to re-evaluate existing beliefs. Certainly, both of these types of students would have (different) reasons to prefer factual content. In the first case, it fits into a worldview in which truth is God-given and unproblematic (see Wittgenstein 1963 for an extensive discussion of these issues). In the second, it would reflect the difficulty the weaker students had in organizing the course information into highly abstract and sometimes counterintuitive conceptual structures. Treating each item of information in such a course as a separate memorizable unit certainly feels like less of a challenge. Will expressed these feelings in regard to his Biology class:

Will: I'm one of these people that if you just present me with facts and the way things are, I'm fine, I can usually get it pretty well. You know, I don't need a lot of examples maybe one will be fine, and it doesn't have to be a long drawn out one unless it's something that I just don't understand at all.

Finally, the isolated and the static nature of facts may imply that the way to learn them is through what Weinstein and Meyer (1991) call repetition strategies—although as I will show in the next section, to do so may be problematic. A student who sees the material in a course as factual in nature may tend to go over the material again and again or use some kind of mnemonic technique unrelated to the meaning of the material. Certainly both Will and Sophie tended to rely more on these techniques than the other two students did, and both of these less successful students consistently tended to see the material in terms of facts. Furthermore, to the extent that the assessment format encourages a factually based understanding of material, this kind of superficial approach will be encouraged. This is not only problematic for learning, but it also can fundamentally mislead students in terms of their prospects in the effort to get grades for reasons that will shortly become apparent.

CONNECTIONS

Will and Sophie showed a similar reluctance to move beyond facts, as did many of the students discussed by Alexander and Dochy

(1994) and Hammer (1994). Yet paradoxically they showed considerable awareness of an overarching structure holding the individual factual units together. Furthermore, it was evident that they knew that links between facts add meaning and at times followed almost naturally from the presentation of the facts. As Will put it, "You know when you go through lecture, and you pay attention, you come with questions like 'Why does that happen like that?' At least I do." All four students found satisfaction in what Greg called "putting pieces together," at least they did when they were interested in the material. More practically, they also appeared to be aware, at some level, that these kinds of links aided memory. Thus, Will associated finding causes and effects to be essential to "code it into my memory," and Sophie actually criticized herself for "laziness" when, while reading Political Science, she found the material boring and became reluctant to put it together. She knew she was missing something important.

Hammer (1994) and Schommer (1994) divide what they consider the structural dimension of knowledge into "pieces" or "isolated" items on the one hand, and "coherent" or "highly interwoven concepts" on the other. The internal structure of infons provides an elegant way to model the source of this structure. Specifically, each relation or argument in an infon is a potential source for relations between it and other infons. These relations consist of cross-infonic links, so to speak, such as sameness, similarity, polarity (existence or nonexistence of the relation), causality, temporality, and so on.

Take a statement such as *The Russian Revolution began with riots*, a simple proposition extracted from Greg's Modern European History class. As a proposition, this idea can be learned as a fact. However, it could also be broken down into the situation-theoretic arguments and relations outlined in the previous section:

> Arguments = Type of situation = revolution
> Location = Russia
> Time = 1917
> Type of individuals = rioters
> Type of situation = riot
> Relation = Initiation

Each of these elements is not unique to this infon but is shared by other (potential) infons. There have been other events in Russia, and these would all share Russia as a location; there have been other revolutions in the world, even other revolutions that began with riots, and so on. This proposition containing Russia can be linked to other propositions containing Russia by a relation of identity of location. The same can be said for other propositions containing revolutions, riots, and revolutions beginning with riots. Moreover, identity is only one possible relation: others include *before, after, cause, led to, prevent,* and so on *ad infinitum.* These relations are informational to those agents who are attuned to them, and they can be codified infonically (and therefore factually). Thus, we can relate the Russian and French Revolutions in the following way (among many other ways):

The Russian Revolution began with riots. The French Revolution began with riots.

The Russian and French revolutions both began with riots.

Each relation on its own may constitute a single infon, and when considered true, it is a fact. However, when two facts are related by more than a small number of arguments, their multiple relations can become more awkward to express as one proposition. Because language has a propositionally based architecture, the more complicated and interactionally connected the facts, the more difficult they are to code linguistically. Specifically, to do so requires embedding one relation inside an argument, and multiple embedding is a hallmark of bad writing.

For instance, in the following, the proposition (C) is achieved by relating (A) and (B), and it is marked with a #, which, following usage in linguistic pragmatics, indicates infelicity:

(A) The Russian Revolution began with a riot.

(B) The Russian Revolution was a response to a rigid autocracy.

(C) #The Russian Revolution began with a riot as a response to a rigid autocracy.

Similarly, when more than two facts are being related at the same time, it is again difficult for the relations to be expressed in a single sentence. This is the case even when each pair of facts might be related simply. One example includes steps in processes, such as DNA to RNA transcription, which Will encountered in his Biology class. In these cases, sometimes even a series of sentences in paragraph format is not an effective way to convey this information. As Will was aware, a diagram would be employed:

Will: I mean how would DNA get to RNA? How would those two transcribe? . . . I just didn't understand how that would work. . . . For something like that they would have diagrams and stuff, and I'd spend time on that.

By the same token, students also used diagrammatic representations of connections themselves. For example, when asked, "What are the five basic steps researchers use in constructing and testing theories" on his Methods midterm, Greg drew the annotated circle shown in Figure 6.1 to directly express the connections in his answer.

In this way Greg captured the relations between the steps as more than just facts, as a structured whole; he received five and a half points out of six, with the half point taken off for some unspecified inadequacy in his description of "conceptualization."

Because these connections can be difficult to express propositionally, they were often communicated indirectly in some way. As a result, students could not just receive them as they did facts, but had to *actively recreate them on the basis of the facts learned.* In these cases, students needed to rely on what Weinstein and Meyer (1986) refer to as elaboration strategies.[5]

Not surprisingly, considering the findings of previous research, the ability to draw out and work with more abstract information was an important factor separating the stronger students, Greg and Carmin, from the weaker ones, Sophie and Will. For example,

Figure 6.1
Greg's Schematic Answer to a Question

+ 5 ½

37. What are the five basic steps researchers use in constructing and testing theories? Very briefly explain each of the steps.

well, often theories are constructed from the springboard of observations which are then generalized (i.e. induction)
And theories are tested by doing research to see if we can confirm the theory w/ observations from the real social world. (i.e. deduction)

These 2 directions are linked in a cycle that joins them together ultimately.

Theory — start of DEDUCTIVE APPROACH - we state relationships between abstract CONCEPTS - indicate direction of causality; a proposition

Conceptualization : "How we will think about concepts" we narrow our concepts to variables that we can measure, non abstract. end up with a hypothesis that states relations between nominally defined terms.

Hypothesis testing
if we determine validity of measures, does it agree w/ hypoth? Is causal relationship the right one expected. Does the data jive w/ the ideas.

Observations
Empirical data collection, field observations, survey analysis; Carrying out the method and organizing it for analysis.

Operationalization
The nitty gritty of how we will measure our variables. Where will we look & what method will we use to measure. Survey, participant observer, etc - refining methodological tools.

although Will was aware that he would sometimes be required to show connections and he was intrinsically interested in them, he did not always look for them when studying. Therefore, when Will was presented with facts alone, he often attempted to memorize them, but not in connected networks or by making reference to his previous knowledge. Instead, he pored over his materials again and again, including his transcriptions of the lectures, spending up to twenty hours preparing for exams on which he would wind up with a B– or C+. Courses such as biology, in which facts were given in large numbers, caused him particular distress, and he was mystified as to how students succeeded at them.

Biology students were asked a total of 160 multiple-choice items between two midterm exams and a final exam. The following are the first four items from the first midterm; they give a sense of the predominantly fact-centered flavor of the tests:

(4) The production of sperm and eggs via meiosis is called:

    a. fertilization   b. initiation

    c. replication   d. gametogenesis

(5) The peripheral nervous system, which is composed of cranial nerves and spinal nerves, can be divided into:

    a. sympathetic nervous system and parasympathetic nervous system

    b. central nervous system and autonomic nervous system

    c. sympathetic nervous system and somatic nervous system

    d. autonomic nervous system and somatic nervous system

(6) Antibiotics are used to treat bacterial infections. Which of the following would NOT respond to antibiotic treatment?

    a. chlamydia   b. vaginitis

    c. papilloma virus-induced genital warts   d. syphilis

(7) The part of the eye that can change its shape to maintain focus is the

    a. lens   b. retina

    c. cornea   d. iris

The biological features (e.g., cornea, meiosis) can be understood as concepts, but because those concepts are embedded in basic propositions in items (4) and (7) they can be approached as facts.[6] Item (5) is only slightly more complex because it asks for two different parts that compose a whole. Only item (6) explicitly calls on the application of conceptual understanding, that what acts on a bacterium will not act on a virus and, by implication, that they are different types of organisms. However, even in this case knowledge of this distinction as a fact (e.g., that *antibiotics do not kill bacteria*) also supplies the answer. Furthermore, the concept of a virus—of an organism consisting of a strand of genetic material inside a protein coat, of its manner of replication, of its inertness outside a host cell, and so on—is absent. The same is true for the concept of an antibiotic. The item demands no expression of why an antibiotic would not work. In this way, these items lend themselves to a solution in terms of simple factual relations. In fact, on this test, I found that all the items could be resolved individually as facts.

This predominance of facts can lead an unwary student into a trap. Although each individual item on the test can be learned as a fact, it is probably impossible to learn as individual pieces *all* the facts needed to do well. The number of facts presented in an introductory science class that may appear on a test is simply too great for students to memorize them individually. This trap is so subtle that a number of researchers have missed it. For example, Crooks (1988), Pintrich and Shrauben (1992), Haas (1994), and Poole (1994) have all suggested that memorizing isolated facts is appropriate when students are tested on factual information.

To avoid the trap, it is important to bear in mind that facts can best be remembered by making connections between them and between new facts and those in prior knowledge. This is the most basic application of schema theory, of course. For test makers, this characteristic of human cognition means that students who produce large numbers of facts are displaying indirectly that they have made appropriate connections. Without such connections they would not be able to remember so many details. This is true even when the connective information itself is not directly displayed. In other words, the knowledge of the connections can be embedded informationally in an assessment through the reproduction of a sufficient number of facts.

For example, although the items shown above could be understood as facts, the answers can also be linked schematically to other knowledge. In item (5), the nervous system can be visualized as a whole. The inappropriateness of antibiotic treatment falls out naturally from an understanding of the taxonomy of life forms. Item (7) can similarly be derived through an understanding of the eye as a system. Even item (4), which intuitively seems to most resist a schematic understanding, can be resolved through a familiarity with the meaning of "gamete" and/or "genesis," which permits the selection of the target choice, *d*. There is undoubtedly a myriad of other ways of arriving at the targets.

A downside of this form of indirect display of connective information is that it is not necessarily known which connections are being employed by the student to determine the correct response. Consequently, which connections have actually been learned is an open question. Even leaving aside such factors as luck or the elimination of unlikely choices, a test-taker may have memorized the particular facts as they are presented on a given item. It is only by viewing an aggregate number of correct responses that it becomes reasonable for the grader to assume that the student has indeed synthesized connective information. Even then, it is not clear which connections have been learned. Evidently, the types of intensive research showing correlations between specific responses and knowledge that characterize standardized tests are not available to the individual college professor.

To return to the student participants, while Will and Sophie appeared to understand that facts are connected, they showed little inclination to put together schemata of course content, and they did relatively poorly on fact-laden exams; they fell right into the trap. The reason was that they were confused about their role in the process. They did not see it as their job to put the facts together unless they were explicitly told to do so. On the contrary, Sophie, for one, strongly believed that teachers should explicitly provide needed connections for students, and she felt cheated when they did not. Will, characteristically less strident, just claimed that "Biology seems to be, at least to me, more facts that, 'OK this is how it is.'" He was not shown any deeper level and he did not look for one.

They were not alone in this belief. Greg felt more or less the same way. He severely criticized his History professor on this point, declaring "her sense of continuity of events" to be "minimal." Her pedagogical failures did not really affect Greg's performance, but they were, he believed, an evasion of her responsibility. The difference between Greg, on the one hand, and Will or Sophie on the other was in how they responded to these perceived instructional failings. Greg consistently understood the need to supply his own connections in the absence of direction. He understood that when a teacher did not provide links between facts, he would have to go out and look for them. He was so conscious of this issue that he named the schemata he created "blueprints" in which "blocks" or facts could be mentally visualized. In this way, Greg, unlike the other students, clearly indicated that he individuated connective information. For his History final, he created an elaborate, multidimensional mental blueprint which he was able to visualize. What follows is a portion of the interview where he described the blueprint:

Greg: I always just think of like a map and movements on the map, then this guy comes up from the Caucasus and then Lenin flees to Norway or Finland, I forget which one, and I'm kinda visualizing this all to keep it in order for me, that's how I . . .

Investig.: But you have like these frames that, pictures of the maps that go by, or is it like a smooth movement from one to the other like a weather map?

Greg: The map stays the same and the things come and go and . . .

Investig.: Do you develop this while you are studying and then . . .

Greg: I develop that and I also develop images like if I'm going through here, I would remember that the women started a revolution or were the ones that started inciting it in March of 1917 because of no food and low morale during the war. The whole society was bummed out, I guess, and I remembered the women marching on Versailles during the French Revolution, and so that was something that had a similar image already created. So that came back a little bit easier, but then it's just a matter of telling a story and just memorizing a story, you know, how does the story go?

Investig.: Right, where does the map come into play in the story?

Greg: Whenever there are movements of things being added or taken away from the scene and in Petrograd in this case, so when, when the Duma, the lower house is waiting for these changes to communism to happen, which is too slow and . . .

Investig.: This is the second revolution?

Greg: This is after the provisional government has been instated. The Germans send Lenin to Petrograd. They supported him, and so I'm imagining in my map you know the Germans sending Lenin, even though I know that's not right, I mean they didn't like send him off on a ship or something. I'm kinda seeing Lenin get the orders or get the tip from the Germans and then go to Petrograd, so I see almost like this, I don't know if you call it an arrow, but there's something flowing from Norway to Petrograd.

By building this complex web of connections, Greg was able to anchor all the pieces of information together and so remember the details he needed for the essay question, even though he did not repeat the schema in paragraph form on that test. By contrast, Will was only able to work with those schemata that his teachers provided him. In International Relations, he was extraordinarily fortunate because Professor Haus provided extensive support of connections by reproducing and selling copies of a set of outlines he used for his own notes and which he displayed on transparencies throughout the lecture. Based on these notes—which Will remarked on appreciatively a number of times—and explicit hints given in class, Will was able to put together a coherent understanding. In Biology and Psychology, where such scaffolding was not provided, he had more difficulties. Sophie, who had no such support in either of her classes, also did poorly. Finally, for Carmin, the material was so easy that it appears most likely that connections simply appeared obvious to her; she had little, if any, need to put them together herself. In the next chapter, I will revisit some of these issues as I discuss how the participants changed the information from a factual to a conceptual format. I will then explore some other reasons for Sophie and Will's difficulties in this matter.

CONCEPTS

As they did with facts, but not with connections, all four respondents referred explicitly to "concepts," and they ranked them higher than facts in terms of value of learning. For instance, Carmin said, "I think a concept you have to learn. A fact that's in front of you, you can memorize." According to Greg, "Not all the words that I read are gonna stick in my head; it's the concepts that are gonna stick in my head." For Will, a goal of rewriting his notes was "thinking about the concepts." Finally, Sophie approved of the use of demonstrations and examples in Chemistry because "looking at those and then reading, I can get that; I can learn concepts better." In these beliefs the students mirrored their instructors, who consistently referred to conceptual knowledge as a major instructional goal.

So it is natural to posit, using the terms of situation theory, that the students and faculty *individuated* rather than merely *discriminated* concepts, much as they did facts, and that assumption was indeed the starting point in my own data analysis. However, it is as dangerous as it is tempting to assume that all uses of a term entail a single common meaning. Even in the theoretical literature, the notion of *concept* has been defined in at least two quite different ways. These include a structural definition as webs of connective information (e.g., Hiebert and Lefevre 1986), and a functional one in terms of how a concept affects other information. It is the functional view that has been proposed in information theory:

A concept is a *type* of internal structure: one whose semantic content, when instantiated, exercises control over system output. When this type of structure (having a content expressible as "x is F") is instantiated relative to some perceptual object s, we have a (*de re*) belief [i.e., belief about something] with the (propositional) content s is F. (Dretske 1981, p. 214)

In other words, concepts are dynamic informational structures with the function of classifying other information, and because they organize information, they are necessary for a cognitive agent to hold a belief. In effect, through their function in interpreting, our concepts shape our beliefs. This functional definition is the one adopted here for empirical and theoretical reasons.

The empirical motivation for adopting a functional understanding lies in the observation that student participants appeared to discriminate between inert, loosely formed webs of connections between infons, which I call connections, and these functional information structures. The following sampling of remarks by all four students illustrates how the two types of information constitute different ways of viewing portions of course content in terms of related tasks. In the case of the connections, the italicized portions deal with links between events, concepts, and facts that are a target of attention in some way:

- *Well this happens so this will happen* and since this happens this will happen. (Will)
- They were all about *organs and hormones and how they work together.* (Will)
- You hadn't heard about gross motor skills, or fine motor skills, definitions? (Investig.) Not as far as *connecting them into the first two years of life.* (Carmin)
- I can understand that *brain cells die off at puberty and that interferes with language learning*, and I can memorize it. (Greg)
- After you get into *the differences of parliamentary and presidential democracies*, it seems like it registered that it's boring. (Sophie)
- It's more of the scientific method and therefore *there's going to be this if you do this.* (Sophie)

By contrast, in the case of concepts, the focus is on some interpretive tool, possibly an explanation as to why some connection is being made. The student can focus on how the tool is used (i.e., a functional definition) or on the tool itself as an object (i.e., a structural one). Even when undertaking a structural view, there remain differences between concepts and connections. First, the function is always latent; second with a concept, unlike a connection, the structure is considered as a whole, with the potential functionality holding it together. Therefore, the attention is more multifaceted and abstract. In the following list, the concepts are italicized:

- One that I find confusing was *Darwin's theories.* Here they asked one concerning which would not be viable to one of his theories. (Will)
- We had to look at this picture and apply *theories that we know.* (Carmin)
- They gave *a mean, a median, and a mode* of a certain population and wanted me to discuss the *significance and central tendency.* (Greg)

- The low *N value*, the population number wouldn't allow for the generalization of the findings to a larger population because they don't have enough in your sample. (Greg)
- He asked what *liberalism* was not, and had a list, a multiple-choice list. (Sophie)
- One of the books is like a step by step, "This is *what an institution is.*" (Sophie)

The distinction is supported theoretically because there are cases of simple propositional structures serving in functional roles just as more complex ones do, meaning that there is a commonality in function despite a difference in structure. Dretske (1981) gives an example of a simple concept in the citation quoted previously; "*x* is *F,*" on its own, is a simple proposition. Another example, one of many that could be culled from the data, is the following pivotal idea from Will's Biology class: *There is only one human species.*

This is a fact that can be memorized, but it can also be treated as a concept because, as will be discussed shortly, it may not be simply learned and stored, but it can be used for further understanding of human biology. Importantly, I found that complex and simple concepts represented substantially different challenges to the students in this study. That is, when the students were faced with simple concepts, the hurdles they had to overcome in their efforts to move the desired information from source to target were different from those when they were faced with complex ones. Also, their needs in interacting with complex concepts further depended on whether they were required to *use* the concept in some way or whether they had to *describe* it in detail, that is, account for its structure. These divisions are shown in Table 6.2, which lists them in the order they are discussed in the remainder of this section and as a function of the perspective adopted.[7] The different difficulties faced by students constitute another motivation for claiming that these differences are real and not just an artifact of analysis.

Table 6.2
Issues in Conceptual Learning and Assessment

Perspective	Simple	Complex
Functional	1.	2.
Structural	N/A	3.

(a) Functional Perspective on Simple Concepts

The simplest concepts take a propositional format, such as the example mentioned from Will's Biology class:

There is only one human species.

Expressed in this way it is a fact, and because Will took it as such, he completely missed its functional possibilities:

Will: I'd actually learn better because then my mind could just focus on what you're saying without the stress of having to get every little tiny detail down on paper like knowing that there's only one human species.

What would make it a concept is if it were used to organize other information (i.e., as input to a belief of some kind). In the case of an introductory course in Human Biology, that type of classification can be important to understand the ways in which humans diverge from one another and the ways we are similar. This potential can be seen more clearly if it is expressed by a noun phrase, as indeed concepts usually are:

the fact that there is one human species

or

the unity of the human species

In that form, it can be used as an argument of other propositions, such as

The fact that there is one human species
implies that race is a social construction.

or

All humans normally have the same number of chromosomes,
which points to the unity of the human species.

It is possible to imagine many other possibilities, a flexibility of use that gives concepts so much of their power. Yet Will never realized the potential of the idea that there is only one human species. Furthermore, the invisibility of this importance to him shows that the ability to distinguish simple concepts from facts may require imagination and considerable knowledge of the context on the part of a student. Essentially, it is an ability to see the promise in a fact to elucidate some other information.

At the risk of following a tangent in the discussion of this matter, it is interesting to note some implications regarding the old dispute between traditional fact-based curricula promulgated by explicit instruction and practice-based approaches that aim primarily to develop critical abilities. Proponents of fact-centered curricula (e.g., Hirsch 1988) have argued in favor of the importance of certain facts on the basis of cultural iconicity and centrality in important schemata. They therefore differentiate facts to be learned from those that need not be learned, and they do so on the basis of connective not conceptual criteria. For example, the name of the oracle at Delphi could be said to matter in *Oedipus Rex* because it figures in so many events in Greek mythology and because of its association with the central figure of Apollo.

By contrast, to differentiate a concept from a fact depends crucially on how the item of information is applied to other knowledge. It is not static and simply stored, but rather it can be applied as a classificatory device to other knowledge. For instance, Delphi might take on conceptual significance if it were used as a way of interpreting the play, perhaps as a sign of the ineluctability of the hero's tragic destiny.

In terms of instruction, it is hard to see how it is possible for a student to be expected to realize the conceptual potential of such an item of information without an opportunity to apply it (i.e., without being encouraged to derive the meaning through active engagement). If the significance of the singularity of the human species for race or for the human genome does not arise explicitly in class and assessments, then finding it depends entirely on the students' initiative. Will happened to remember that fact, and he chose the target on the corresponding item on the test. However, he lost out on an opportunity for his knowledge of biology to shape his view of his social world and of humanity in general, and is not developing that ability one of the most important rationales for a biology course for nonmajors? Are only the most creative of students to benefit from such courses? Also, are those students whose previous training has not taught them to be on the lookout for concepts and what to do with them to be excluded from success in these classes? A heavy emphasis on facts and connections does not recognize the importance of concepts, and so this method is not designed to teach students creative engagement with information.

On the other hand, the conceptual potential of the unity of the human species, like that of Delphi, depends just as crucially on the student's awareness of other facts about humans and biology. In order to apply the knowledge that there is one human species, Will must know a considerable amount about the context of application, biological and social. By the same token—returning to the example from Theatre—the conceptual potential of the Oracle at Delphi depends on a broad understanding of Greek mythology (e.g., facts such as that Delphi was sacred to Apollo and what else happened there). Had Carmin's knowledge of Greek mythology generally been broader, she probably would have gotten the quiz question right. More important, she would have understood the play better. Conceptual potential thus also requires an ample knowledge base, implying that it is not sufficient to only teach students techniques for applying concepts for understanding. Critical thinking, the ability to analyze, and knowledge of the importance of concepts are not enough. Learners must also be aware of the more static background knowledge to apply them.

What these observations amount to is an argument in favor of a principled eclecticism in pedagogy of the type proposed by the New London Group (1996/2000). Such eclecticism is not a hodgepodge of instructional techniques but a clearly thought-out application of instructional objectives and methods appropriate for sophisticated curricular goals. This plan can include when to look for and apply concepts, and it always depends on the student's knowledge background and needs.

To return to the main thread of this discussion, it is important to note that faculty gave the highest importance to applications of concepts when ennunciating their pedagogical goals. All the faculty interviewed specifically mentioned the need for students to apply concepts in their courses. Professor Haus, Will's International Relations instructor, wanted them to be able to apply what he called "theories, paradigms, concepts, and frameworks" to concrete situations in world politics. Mr. Hill, his Psychology Writing instructor, and Professor Tomko, Greg's Statistics professor, wanted to see applications of the concepts brought up in their classes in assessments. Professor Riordan of Carmin's Theatre class wanted her students to use concepts to improve their understanding of the plays that they would see. Sophie's Chemistry instructor, Professor Thomas, even included applications of chemical principles to such mundane tasks as taking oil stains out of clothes.[8]

For his part, Will was not unaware of the need to apply concepts; he actually talked about them almost twice as often as any of the other informants and more than ten times as often as Sophie, who talked about them the least. He also had considerable insight into what he needed to succeed: an instructional approach that explicitly highlighted and clarified concepts. He thus reported, "If they give a concept and basically what it's about, I can pretty much bring it into what it's actual functions are, and I can see how it would correlate to something in the real world." When he got that help, as he did in International Relations, he did well. However, when left on his own, he was unclear about which elements of a concept to apply and how to pick concepts out from the mass of other information he encountered. I leave a deeper discussion of this issue to the next chapter.

(b) Functional Views of Complex Concepts

Complex concepts include theories, paradigms, and frameworks, as Professor Haus enumerated, all of which can be characterized structurally as consisting of specified networks of propositions. If the simple concepts are structurally facts, complex ones are structurally connections; however, unlike other connections, they are well defined. In other words, the connections between two or more events, processes, or facts may be multiple and amorphous. By contrast, a concept usually has a single, though perhaps complex and contested, definition.

This very intricacy reduces the danger that these concepts could be mistaken for anything else, and the challenges I observed indeed lay in other areas. Will's trouble applying theories in his writing, for instance, involved keeping the applications simple and direct and, in particular, not trying to do too much or use too many concepts at the same time:

Will: I always lose points for not like explaining my argument as well as I should. . . . I was talking about using the Catell and Horn theory, and then I was talking about using something else, and he was like, "Just make sure not to wear yourself down in any part; explain everything." So I just narrowed it down to the Catell and Horn theory on Monday and just wrote that. So then I had to spend a lot of time with the Catell and Horn theory and deciding exactly how I wanted to state it, and then I looked at other theories in intelligence because I was still going to try to put some others in, but I just ran out of room, and it just ended up being the Catell and Horn theory.

Paradoxically, some of Will's troubles reflected his own interest in the subject. He did not understand assignments narrowly but was always curious about "how the mind works." So he would try to apply concepts he encountered in other areas and ended up focusing more on the phenomenon being analyzed than on the theory he needed to explicate:

Will: When I hear something like a theory or something like that, I might not know its specifics but I know how the theory works, and I can relate that to my own and other people's actions. "OK well maybe he acted that way because you know," and kinda do correlations with that. So I might not know the exact definitions but I know what it basically means, and I do a lot more with bringing that into my every-day life.

In effect, this lack of a complete understanding meant that Will could only explain phenomena partially. A severe case can be seen in the following short-answer item, which highlighted concept application and on which he received only one out of five points.

(8) Imagine that the correlation coefficient between automobile price and gas mileage is 0.3 and the correlation coefficient between automobile size and gas mileage is −0.8. What can you tell me about the relationship between automobile price, size, and gas mileage?

Will's answer:

The price of the car and gas mileage are connected and relation between auto size and gas mileage also are connected. The automobile price, size and gas mileage are all corrilated [*sic*]. The variance in the stats make the variance significant.

Applications of theories were tightly entangled with issues of criteria for and methods of assessment. An extended essay on a concept or phenomenon, such as Will's Catell and Horn example, is far less scaffolded than an exam essay item that asks a student to apply a specified concept in a specific way, such as the above question. That type of question is, in turn, less limited and structured than a single conceptual application asked for in a multiple-choice item. Naturally, when the application of a concept is requested in a less structured way, there are more opportunities for a student to go off in the wrong direction. On the other hand, there is more wiggle room for students to respond by supplying applications they may have memorized or do understand but that may not be exactly those anticipated by the instructor. In these cases, professors sometimes had trouble determining the scoring since the student could claim that the question was unclear. The deliberate employment of this vague approach is called "bullshitting."

Multiple-choice test items, as the most constrained form of response, cause their own difficulties largely because their propositional structure cannot give sufficient scope for a real expression of the uses of a concept. Therefore, the application of concepts has to be performed piecemeal, with items asking about the validity of one or another consequence of a concept without reference to any other consequence or complicating contextual factors. At best, they involve propositions related to the target concepts.

The most common way that was done was to use the concept in an item stem to explain a fact or facts about the world. The following example, culled from Sophie's Political Science midterm, is typical in that respect and should be immediately recognizable to anyone at all familiar with American multiple-choice exams:

(9) P[roportional] R[epresentation] laws tend to:

    (a) favor large parties disproportionately

    (b) promote more stable parties

    (c) promote more stable government

    (d) promote a greater choice for voters

This particular case is interesting because just before the exam, Sophie was able to provide a passable description of the main issue involved:

Sophie: A SMDP, a Single Member District Priority [*sic*], that is a type of electoral system . . . more likely used a two–major-party system. Whereas proportional representation is used in a multiparty system.

Sophie's association of SMDP with a two-party system and PR to a multiparty system should have been enough for her to select the target *d* if she had made a relatively straightforward inference: Multiple parties provide greater choice than two parties. However, she not only missed this item during the test, but the week after she got the test back she appeared unable to explain why she got it wrong, even as she was going over the test with us. Instead, she blamed the teaching assistant in charge of the recitation section, who, she claimed, had managed to confuse her. In so doing, she added a face-saving rationalization commonly used by the two weaker students: that a lot of classmates made the same error.

Sophie: It was one of the things [the TA] hadn't explained real well. She doesn't do a very good of job of explaining things, but it came down to, oh, what's it called, SMDP, Single Member District Plurality, and two party systems and stuff like that and the difference between SMDPs and PRs, and which electoral system would be what kind of party system. It was very complex and she just really screwed the whole thing up. A lot of people got those kinds of questions wrong.

A better explanation is that she treated the item as a fact that she just didn't know rather than trying to make elementary inferences based on what she did know. Since she felt she did not know it, she guessed, wrongly as it turned out. She was more successful in the following chemistry item, which illustrates an alternative structure for testing concepts.

(10) Which statement is false about the following reaction?

$$2 \ Al(s) + 3 \ Br2 \ (l) \longrightarrow 2AlBr3 \ (s)$$

(a) this is a combination reaction.
(b) bromine is gaining electrons.
(c) aluminum is oxidizing.
(d) aluminium bromide is a solid.
(e) aluminum is gaining electrons

Whereas in the item on proportional representation, the concept under scrutiny is in the stem, in this chemistry item, five concepts are distributed between the stem and choices. They include (1) *reaction* and (2) *electron shell structure*—of aluminum and bromine—in the stem and (3) *combination reaction* (4) *gaining electrons,* and (5) *oxidation* in the choices. In addition, there is what I call *metainformational* information involving the ability of students to read formulas, including as a red herring the use of (s) and (l) to indicate the irrelevant states of matter, solid and liquid, respectively. To make matters even more opaque, the whole item is couched in negative terms, so that the test taker has to take care not to simply pick *a* as the first positive response encountered.

At least at first glance, it would appear that a test taker would need to know something about the meaning of all or at least most of these concepts to realize that when aluminum combines with bromine, it does not gain electrons as the target, choice *e,* states. In addition, students would also need to control the metainformational factors (i.e., the meaning of the formulas) to provide access to the concepts being tested. If either type of knowledge is missing, the student, it appears, cannot resolve the item. These two ways of going wrong make it impossible to determine which type of information led a student who misses this item into error.

What is even more confusing is that it is not clear which concepts are actually needed to solve the problem because it is also possible to do so using a much simpler combination of metalinguistic and conceptual factors, as indeed Sophie reported doing. All the test taker really needs to know is that the element on the left in a compound—any compound—loses electrons relative to its elemental state and the one on the right gains them. It is also possible to determine the item if the test taker knows that metals lose electrons and nonmetals gain them when the two combine, and that bromine is not a metal. Both are undoubtedly important facts in chemistry, but the existence of multiple routes to the target and multiple ones to distractors make it hard to say which specific concept(s) the item is designed to measure and whether it actually measures them. In its conceptual diffuseness, this item was typical of at least one-quarter of the items on the exam.

A more successful strategy for measuring application of concepts found on respondents' multiple-choice exams was to set up hypothetical situations and ask the students to apply conceptual knowledge to them. The following examples are from Greg's Sociology Methods and his Statistics midterms, respectively:

(11) You have a theory which states that perceived competition of minorities is a cause of the extent of prejudice in a city and that economic hardship is also a cause of the extent of prejudice in a city. This is an example of

    a. mutual causation   c. illogical reasoning

    b. multiple independent causation   d. spurious causation

(12) In a sample of 107 adults a researcher finds that the mean age is 33 years old, the median age is 43 years old, and the standard deviation is 4.3 years. This distribution of age is:

    a. negatively skewed   c. positively skewed

    b. symmetric   d. bimodal

In the first example, the assessed concept is found in the choices, together with three possible distractor alternatives, and it must be applied to the information in the stem. In the second, concepts are distributed between the item and choices. The informational format in these cases is far more straightforward. Although the application of the concept remains piecemeal, the fictitious nature of the situation prevents the resulting proposition from being treated as a fact or connection that can be memorized. Still, it should be pointed out that the use of more than one concept in items and stem means that the student needs to know all the concepts to avoid at least some guessing. Therefore, when the student makes an error, it still may not be possible to determine which concept caused the slip up, and therefore which concept the student does not know.

The exams were divided in terms of their choice of informational formats. On the Sociology Methods midterm, nineteen out of thirty-five items involved applications of concepts to fictitious situations. On the Statistics exam, the proportion was even higher, twenty-four out of thirty. Nevertheless, in spite of their far greater (face) validity, this type of item was rare on the respondents' other tests. There were none on Carmin's Human Development midterms (out of forty) or Sophie's Political Science midterm (out of thirty), and there was only one each on Will's Biology exam (out of forty) and Sophie's Chemistry (out of thirty) exam. The reasons for the selection of a less transparent type of item on these tests is not clear; it is certainly not difficult to imagine the construction of imaginary situations in which to apply concepts in these subjects.

Writing, as I said earlier, provides a less constrained way of assessing the application of concepts than multiple-choice items do. Although Carmin had little good to say about her Human Development class, one essay question on the final did provoke her respect because she was able to write out an answer that made her think. It involved a picture of a poor child in an African village and asked students to apply five concepts studied in class to that child. This item is discussed in detail in the next chapter. In other questions, students were given a choice of concepts and asked to supply specific applications, including nature versus nurture, deficit versus difference, and continuous versus discontinuous development.

Similarly, Professor Riordan, Carmin's Theatre lecturer, insisted on including some writing in her class. She assigned this work in the form of essay test questions included on the midterm and final exams in spite of the difficulty with coordinating fair and reliable grading of writing in a "megaclass" of up to 400 students. Will's Professor Haus similarly believed that without writing it would be difficult to achieve course objectives regarding concepts:

> *Haus*: You ought to be able to make the case for or against free trade, you ought to be able to distinguish between ... NUT, nuclear utilization theory, and MAD, mutual assured destruction. You ought to be able to contrast the liberal structuralist and mercantile theories of economic development; you ought to be able to take those theories and then apply them.

He asked students this type of question in an essay format on the midterm and final exams, in addition to the multiple-choice portion. In fact, whatever Will's opinion on the application of concepts in that exam, he did far better on the essay, on which he got full credit, than he did on the multiple-choice portion, on which he lost fourteen out of sixty points. Unfortunately, I was unable to review this exam.

Even Greg's fact-centered history course had essay questions that led Greg to concept application, although this time to his own disadvantage. Students were asked to describe the features of Napoleon's reign, and Greg used the concept of "police state" to describe his regime. The instructor took off points, with the comment that Greg had been too "hard on Napoleon," because "a police state was not his idea." Had Greg not evaluated Napoleon in terms of this concept but simply recounted events of history and standard interpretations lifted from the text, he probably would not have lost these points. He used that kind of straight chronicle on another question on the French Revolution and got a perfect score.

(c) Structural View of Complex Concepts

A structural view of a concept contrasts with concept application because it involves an expectation of some kind of description of the components of the concept. In a sense, this view is similar to connective information, but the functional dimension remains latent since, as with any tool, the structure serves the function. Structural approaches to concepts predominated in assignments in both introductory science courses, Will's Human Biology course and Sophie's Chemistry course. In fact, all but two of the thirty-four questions on the Chemistry midterm and all but one (the example involving the antibiotics discussed in the previous section) of the forty items on the Biology midterm were structural descriptions. Students frequently referred to such items as "definition questions," but they were partial definitions at best. As in the functional questions, the multiple-choice formats used on these exams required a piecemeal approach, which means that each individual item is a statement of a fact about the concept(s) in question. Examples include

(13) In which of the following sequences are the prefixes of the metric system listed in order of increasing size? [*sic*]
a) nano, micro, deci   b) centi, milli, deci   c) milli, deci, centi
d) micro, kilo, deci   e) nano, milli, micro

(14) What structures form the ectoderm during development?
a) skin and nervous tissue   b) bone   c) muscle
d) internal organs such as the lungs and liver

In the first item, from Chemistry, a series of candidate concepts in the choices is matched to a description in the stem, while in the second, from Biology, the concept is found in the stem, and it is matched to candidate descriptions in the choices. Other examples, which will be discussed in reference to particular points, were more complex, distributing the concepts between stem and choices.

It is sometimes the case that the mixture of application versus description is presented on an assessment in such a way that it is hard to blame the student for becoming confused as to what information should be displayed. Exhibit A comes from one of Carmin's two Human Development midterms, which were virtual treasure troves of items that illustrate the myriad ways that multiple-choice testing can go wrong.

(15) Which of the following best describes Vygotsky's zone of proximal development?

(a) cognitive distance between acquired development and level of potential development under guidance

(b) speed of movement through ZPD is influenced by instructor's voice, personal motivation, familiarity with the tasks

(c) role of adults who interact with preschool children is to use language to facilitate the child's learning of new ideas

(d) all of the above

Carmin chose *a*, but the target was *d*. Carmin did not comment on the semantic contradiction between a "best describes" item and an "all of the above" target (which actually appeared in three other items as well). Instead, she defended her choice in terms of the structural aspect of the concept, which she believed was required by the verb *describe*:

Carmin: I thought that zone of proximal development, the best description of it would be *a*, but *b* and *c* are also factors in it, not so much a description. I recognize that they have something to do with the concept, but I don't think they are descriptions of the concept.

It is hard to argue with Carmin's point here. Had Carmin complained, the instructor might have had a difficult time defending her test, and she said that she would have complained if the item had threatened her overall course grade in the class.

Again, as with applications, more comprehensive definitions required writing. Will again proved sometimes unable to do the kind of analysis needed to answer these questions on his Psychology tests. Asked for a definition of "statistically significant" on a short essay question on his Psychology midterm, he wrote a kind of a scattering of thoughts complete with spelling errors, rushed writing, and incorrect use of signs, as shown:

(16) Statistically Significant: a find is Statistically significant if there is one or more stimulus being tested and the covary with each other.

Ex. Covary $1 + -1$ is significant

but

if they covary 0 there is no significance.

In going over this question in an interview, Mr. Hill, the instructor, expressed the opinion that "he had a lot of stuff in his head. It hadn't really crystallized, and so he just sort of dumps a bunch of thoughts, broken down here, with the answers. You see this stuff is related to significance but it's not significance; it's like all the statistics is thrown together." However, Will had gone over some of the material orally with Hill only a day before the test, and it seemed to Hill that he had a more or less reasonable grasp. So he also hypothesized that Will "just froze" on this test. The errors in his writing could certainly be construed as evidence of a high level of anxiety.

Nevertheless, Will never gave this excuse in our interviews with him, and there were times when he would explain a concept in an interview in similarly disorganized terms without being under any pressure. The following example from his best class—Political Science—seems somewhat extreme in its confusion, but it was one of a number I could have provided. It is particularly interesting because Will appeared completely unaware of the inconsistency and even incomprehensibility of his explanation:

Will: I can sum up this stuff pretty quickly actually. This stuff here was made by the democracy by a different name. It's talking about of course democracy, and what Russia falling and the really great power well Communist power, that's the word I was looking for. It's shaken up I guess a lot of the international structures and politics and a lot of people. I guess one of the questions and has been for a while, "is," like, "democracy safe for the world?" They say the democratic countries don't fight as much of course among themselves where these other governments you know are fighting with everybody.

Still at other times Will could be painfully aware of his troubles with getting the concepts consciously organized for recounting on a test or paper. Referring to yet another class, Biology, he said, "You have to really think about it, but even with thinking about it and looking at [Darwin's] theories in four different classes, I still had a little trouble, and I still don't know if I got it right." My best interpretation of this contradictory data is that Will understood that he could learn a concept as a well-defined informational structure, but how to do so remained a bit vague for him.

Another type of difficulty arose when students were unaware that they were supposed to recount a description of a concept. This appears to be the case with the following Statistics exercises devoted to the interpretation of data given in Greg's class.

(17) You are given data for 12 Tecumseh residents on the number of times each week they read the Tecumseh Universal newspaper.[9] These data are as follows:

   3 5 5 0 0 1 2 6 5 3 1 2

   From this information calculate the mean, median, mode, range, and standard deviation of the number of times each week these Tecumseh residents read the Tecumseh Universal.

   Interpret all of these measures as they describe the typical tendency and the dispersion of the number of times each week these Tecumseh residents read the Tecumseh Universal newspaper. Do the different measures lead you to different conclusions about the central tendency and the dispersion of the distribution of the number of times each week these Tecumseh residents read their city's newspaper? If they do, describe how and why they lead you to different conclusions.

Greg, perhaps because of his irregular attendance, did not realize that the expectations included a structural description of the statistical measures involved in addition to applications explicitly requested in the prompt. Therefore, when he got back his exercise, he found he lost points because of his lack of explicit description of *median, mean,* and so on. He had not seen the need to define such basic notions, an activity he thought of as busy work. A higher-level approach, on his view, would more closely approximate what he understood to be a real statistical analysis, in which, he felt, basic definitions would not be included. Unfortunately, Dr. Tomko did not agree with this rationale. Her response to my restating of Greg's argument was as follows:

Tomko: I guess there is some minor way in which . . . it is at a higher level, but in some ways that in and of itself means that you are not done telling us that you understand the more basic material; you're not conveying how you understand.

Investig.: Let me play devil's advocate. The basic material is concepts, and this shows that I understand the concepts.

Tomko: My response to that would be that you never showed me that you understand the concept of what the mean is and what the mean tells you as compared to what the median tells you about the variable here, which is newspaper readership, because you never tell me what the median is telling you about how much people read newspapers, and what the mean is telling you about how much they read newspapers. You are just stating what those data are.

Investig.: And if I'm showing that the mean is more sensitive to outliers, then aren't I showing what the mean is? Aren't I showing an understanding of what the mean is?

Tomko: You are showing an understanding of one of the properties of the mean, but not what the mean is.

As Professor Tomko's argument suggests, one rationale for requiring a structural description is that it deals with the functional possibilities a concept has. A single employment of a concept to a particular data set may only give "a property" of that concept. The expression of the complete structural description shows the evaluator that the student knows the whole concept and could presumably apply it in other circumstances, in other ways. A second rationale for expecting a structural account is related to the nature of assessment, which according to Professor Tomko, "is to convey to the instructor that they understood the material as presented to them."

This last point puts into relief the contrast between Greg's and Professor Tomko's opinions and unexpectedly captures another fault line between traditional educational approaches and more naturalistic ones. In traditional views, a test is unambiguously and overtly a display of knowledge. In naturalistic pedagogies, such as cognitive apprenticeships and others based on legitimate peripheral participation (Brown, Collins, and Duguid 1989; Lave and Wenger 1991), students are supposed to approximate actual practice in the "real world." In normal professional practice, a concept may be employed in limited ways in each case that it is applied. Therefore, students who are learning by doing are not required to employ that concept comprehensively in every application; nor are they required to give a complete decontextualized descriptive account. The displays of information are as indirect as the instruction is. Thus, a range of latent functionalities and the structural properties of the concept may never be touched upon. Professor Tomko's point could be construed then as a criticism of practice-based approaches to the extent that the knowledge so derived and examined is less complete and reflective.

Finally, conceptual descriptions were often combined with displays of facts or connections on assessments. An example includes a short essay question form Greg's Methods class:

(18) How does a nominal definition differ from an operational definition?

This question is expressed in the form of connections, but in fact it requires a look at a number of aspects of the concepts involved.

Thus, Greg's answer lost a mere half point out of six because he did not mention, as the grader wrote, "Abstract/unobservable vs. concrete/observable." Other than that, the answer gives a sense of Greg's style:

Good question! Was thinking about this the other day. What I could figure out was that a nominal definition is the result of conceptualizing your broad abstract concept in your theory to a more narrow and measurable variable used in the hypothesis. You *define* your concept to be a specific type or case and select the dimensions you wanna deal w/. Example) concept is SES but nominally you define it as *achieved social status*.

The operational definition concerns how you will measure your variable. It involves a methodology and a population—getting even more specific. Ex) SES has the operational definition in a certain study of acquired economic status *as measured by* income levels of Hispanic women based on questionnairre [*sic*] data.

To grade this question, a rubric (perhaps unwritten and informal) must be used to see whether or not the student has displayed the required aspects of the concepts in question. The remainder of the features, appropriate style, spelling, and so on, may not affect the grade even if the grader finds them irritating or a relief from the dry prose generally found in such answers.

Summary of Issues Presented by Concepts

The differentiation between structural and functional aspects of concepts clearly caused difficulties for study participants, as did the need to distinguish between facts and concepts, particularly in assessments. Although I cannot make claims regarding how often these issues might arise, working on these distinctions with students provides a potentially important way of helping them succeed. By the same token, one way to improve student performance might be to diagnose areas of confusion and provide overt instruction in those areas. Finally, it would be useful for faculty to explicate those aspects of their curriculum that are conceptual, and which dimensions of concepts they are aiming at. Awareness of these principles would allow faculty to consciously tailor their assessments accordingly.

PROCESSES

Whatever the differences between them, facts, connections, and concepts all involve declarative knowledge. Although this kind of knowledge predominated, there were times when students encountered, worked with, and were required to display procedural knowledge. The simplest case was the knowledge of steps in carrying out procedures, referred to here as *processes*. This type of information was most common in statistics and methods classes, although it is presumably important in other courses that these students were not taking.[10]

Again there was evidence that students discriminated and sometimes even individuated this type of information when they had classes that called for it. Carmin, for instance, referred to this kind of information as "memorizing steps," implying a parallel between processes and facts, which she also "memorized." She furthermore contrasted processes with principles, which are discussed in the next section, much as she contrasted facts and concepts. Similarly, Greg complained about what he was being required to do in his Statistics recitation, much as he complained about the fact-centered History class:

> *Greg*: A lot of those assignments . . . seemed to be, "Are you computer literate?" "Can you figure out how to get to a certain screen and pull up a certain chart and print it out?" and/or "Can you construct this chart?" and so in that respect it doesn't necessarily mean that you understand it, but you follow the directions that they gave out in recitation, and I've tried to avoid doing that just because when I was reading these explanations . . . they were so boring!

Greg's lack of interest became a problem for him because he had never bothered to learn how to enter the results of calculations on a statistics exercise and so instead he penciled in the results by hand. He lost points because, as he put it, "They wanted the computer to do it."

The simplest way of modeling processes in situation-theoretic terms employs Israel and Perry's (1991, p. 158) notion of "success conditions," defined as the conditions necessary for a result designed into a system. They illustrate this notion by describing its role in the operation of a mousetrap. The goal of a mousetrap is to kill mice. The success condition (P), shown below, indicates the necessity for the blade to hit a mouse and not, say, a toe:

(P) The thing in the path of the blade is a mouse.

Students in a task requiring processes imagine themselves in the role of a conscious "device" designed to obtain some result. They must provide information that represents the accomplishment of one or more of the success conditions required for the accomplishment of that goal. Specifically, they must display knowledge of a single targeted step of a routine. These objectives included completion of parts of statistical analyses as well as using a computer for tasks, as was the case of Greg's missing computer-generated numbers. Other potential examples might involve steps in writing a computer program or parts of building an engineering model. All these cases would provide examples of processes whenever students are required to supply a necessary step or series of steps that form components of the larger routine. It would be interesting to see future research on students taking these courses.

In this study, only Carmin and Greg had a course in which processes played any significant role, and so there are few data to report. In this limited data, two issues stand out. The first is the importance, not surprisingly, of practice. The second was that although processes could be remembered without the conceptual back-up provided by principles, it was easier when done with such knowledge, much as facts were better acquired in terms of concepts and connections. Both these points are made in the following self-criticism by Greg:

Greg: Now, I didn't practice this stuff very well. I only practiced it insofar as doing the assignments. I never did any problems. So putting it into practice might be a downfall when it comes to the exam because I can explain it; I can think about it, but when it comes to the time/pressure situations, I have to act like a robot, and that's . . . what I always have been able to do—study something so well, that I could do it without thinking about it. And I think that is interesting because that's working against what you're supposed to be learning how to do, to think about things. I guess it's good if it just becomes second nature, and you can still understand it, but if you start doing things, procedures, operations, because of a pattern but don't understand the pattern, you can have a high performance but still not know what is going on, so I am still gonna do problems and practice because I don't want to be all stressed out in the exam when she gives us questions in different forms. I kind of want to know it like the back of my hand so I don't have this stress.

In Greg's Statistics class, exams were devoted for the most part to declarative information, particularly concepts, but they included some processes. Exercises, which also were graded, involved how to actually do statistics but included some concepts. The example of an exercise on page 97 included the processes of calculating statistical measure of central tendency with data relating to newspaper readership in addition to descriptions and applications of statistical concepts. The following exercise was more typical because it emphasized processes:

(19) As an educational researcher, you are interested in the relationship between the number of hours students study for a final examination and the grade they receive on the final exam. You perform a regression analysis on a sample of 60 students and find the following results:

$a = 20$ $b = 15$ standard error of $b = 6$ $r = 0.83$

Write out the regression equation for these sample results.

Interpret the meaning of the values of a and b for these results.

Test for the significance of the relationship between the number of hours studied for a final exam and the grade on the final exam at an alpha of .01. State your conclusions.

Interpret the value and meaning of a measure of the strength of the relationship between the number of hours studied for a final exam and the grade on the final exam.

Such questions largely involve the selection of steps that have to be memorized in series. Rarer examples could be found on exams, such as cases where Greg had to determine specific quantities and measures based on data sets supplied. Some were so simple as to appear to be measuring basic math skills or the ability to read a chart. In one example, test takers were given a frequency distribution of raw data on individuals who consumed various numbers of drinks per week and were asked to calculate a percentage of those who consumed the most. This was basic arithmetic. Others were more complex:

We know that the variable occupational prestige (a scale ranging from 0–100) is normally distributed with a population mean of 53 and a population standard deviation of 12. Use this information to answer questions [18, 19, and 20].

(20) The percentage of persons with occupational prestige scores between 29 and 77 is:

a. 95.44%   c. Impossible to determine from the information given

b. 68.26%   d. 50%

(21) The median occupational prestige is:

a. unknown   b. 68.26   c. 53   d. 50

(22) If the variable *age* is also normally distributed, the population mean and population standard deviation (in years) must be:

a. 53 and 12   c. 65 and 3.5

b. any possible number of years of age   d. none of the above

There were only seven out of thirty-five multiple-choice items on the midterm that dealt with processes, although they formed a significant component of essay questions.

PRINCIPLES

It is one thing to learn success conditions in routines individually or even in series; we need to make sure that a mouse is in the way of the blade for the trap to work. It is quite another to understand that behind that and the remaining success conditions lie the laws of physics and biology that make the gory goal achievable. These are the *principles* that enable a mousetrap to work. Students are not, of course, mechanical devices when they perform processes, and so the employment of principles engages their intelligence. Just as there is a parallel between facts and processes, there is also one between concepts and principles. In fact, principles might be understood as the application of concepts to processes as opposed to facts. Greg discussed both the similarities and differences between concepts and principles as he discussed the nature of statistics:

Greg: [Statistics is] more of an analytical puzzle, it's a bunch of steps that you memorize and the steps can be logically tied together if you understand an overarching concept, and that makes it easier to do the steps. But they can also be memorized for their own sake and that's just imitation. If you put your right hand up, I put my right hand up; if you put your left hand up, I put my left hand up, and then I can do it without you showing me, and I can learn a whole dance that way but not know maybe the symbolism that is involved in this dance, or I might not know that it's supposed to represent a monster in the dance.

Investig.: Or know when to do the dance.

Greg: Right, I just do the chi-square. The analytical puzzle part is really different because it doesn't necessitate that I know the overarching reason for doing it all. However, I figured it out for all my statistics, for the f-test, the chi-square, when to use them, difference of means test, and that made me feel like I knew it. Once I figured out the overarching reason and the rationale behind each of those tests, it wasn't just a bunch of blocks anymore, it was the entire blueprint. I wasn't just saying OK, block one then block two then block three, I had the whole blueprint.

In spite of his problems in Statistics, Greg did feel Professor Tomko valued the kind of thoughtfulness that marks information as principled and described her tests as "fair" because they required students to figure out which statistical operations to use. In Greg's Statistics midterm, principles were interrogated in five multiple-choice questions and formed a considerable portion of essay questions.

Unfortunately, the results concerning the use, learning, and testing of principles, like those involved with processes, are rather sketchy in this study. The subject awaits further exploration in research involving courses in areas that depend heavily on procedural knowledge.

METAINFORMATION

The term *metainformation* is a way of referring to the *form* of an information display as itself informational. Grammatical accuracy; generic rules; and chemical, mathematical, and statistical symbols are all metainformation. This category is included because students' grades depended not only on interactions with the content but also interactions with the format used to convey that content. This type of information display appeared most prominently but not exclusively in written language, and the bulk of the literature that has dealt with what I am calling metainformation is concerned with writing. Nevertheless, although I maintain that focus of attention on writing issues here, I believe an exclusive concern with writing distorts the basic issue, which is how students demonstrate knowledge of norms of expression generally. Academic literacy is not synonymous with academic writing; it is multimodal.

An example already discussed includes the use of chemical formulas, which were a major factor in success in that class. In fact, there were times when students had problems with metainformation that were unrelated to language at all, as when Greg penciled in results that were supposed to have been computer generated. Because he used the wrong form rather than content, his failing could be seen as metainformational in nature as well as process related. Case-study students were also expected to produce and understand numerical symbols, diagrams, and oral language in class presentations.

Still, writing predominates, and so I will concentrate on it here, in particular examining a few areas where an informational approach may get at problems that have not received much attention or have resisted solution in the literature. One involves norms.

Many composition theorists take an antinormative stance because they see norms as mechanisms for dominant groups to maintain hegemony. Even Delpit (1995), despite advocating explicit teaching of norms of standard language and discourse to disenfranchised students, has essentially accepted this premise. She just points out that these students need to learn what she calls "codes of power," as if the only function of these forms were to provide or deny access to resources. She discusses no rationale or function for norms beyond this resource-control function. Nevertheless, the fact is that norms of language, like those of other human behaviors, are universal, and moreover every overthrow of one set of norms has resulted in the imposition of a another. For this reason, it seems extremely unlikely that only those who exercise disproportionate control of resources are stakeholders in norms.

In other words, without denying the role of norms in maintaining social inequality, there is something improbable about the idea that they are foisted upon society only for that purpose. To say that norms of language only preserve the current social order is thus not that different from asserting that norms of property solely serve to preserve the unequal distribution of wealth. They certainly do have that function, but they do quite a bit more, and it is unlikely that those on the losing end of the struggle for resources would be better off if they did not exist.

One reason for the inevitability of norms has been proposed by Bartsch (1987), who claims that norms are a way of creating a predictability in human social interactions. What norms do, she argues, is to assure default interpretations of behavior in specific circumstances. Norms of communication thus create the predictability needed for information exchanges to function. Some people may abuse their control of that function, admittedly, but that does not take away from the fact that norms of language and other forms of communication are useful to everyone, though not equally so.

One potential objection to this proposal is that linguistic communication often occurs seamlessly even in some situations of norm variation, such as in interdialect communication (Newman 1996). It would seem that the intuitive notion that we all need to have the same spelling or grammar to understand each other is false. Situation theory, on the other hand, provides a way of understanding normative requirements not in terms of avoidance of literal ambiguities but in terms of intertextuality.

If we think of texts as situations, then according to the relation theory of meaning (see p. 25) any relations between uniformities or features in one text and those of another will be (potentially) meaningful. Recall that, according to this theory, information arises through the existence of relations between uniformities in one situation and those in another. One obvious relation is that of sameness, and therefore when two texts share the same linguistic feature, that feature constitutes an intertextual linkage. By the same token, when two texts have different features where the same one might be expected—different words with the same denotation, different grammatical forms with the same function, or different spellings for the same word—those differences too are meaningful.

It can be said that the greater the convergences in form, the higher the number of relations of similarity, the more tightly bound the texts are. Conversely, the fewer the convergences, the looser the bonds are. Formal similarities between texts could then be understood as creating clusters of implicit intertextual links between all texts of that genre. When someone encounters a new text, the formal similarities and differences may cause them to place that text closer to or farther from other texts that they have previously encountered. In this way, formal features allow readers and hearers to place a text in this linguistic galaxy. Norms provide rules for which features belong with which cluster of texts, and so guide the writer in correct placement. The issue goes beyond prescriptive norms of writing because there are clear normative expectations for socializing in various circumstances, for pillow talk, for commercial transactions, and so on. In the end, this approach sees the formal choices found in a text as constituting information about genre and register. A student therefore needs to learn representational conventions so that they can use formal features to accurately indicate the genres of the text they are producing. Again, the metainformational principle is not exclusively linguistic but applies across modalities, including those using graphics, symbols, space, sound, gestures, and numbers.

This very text can be used as an illustration; one way to understand the forms encountered here is to see that they largely follow some preestablished arbitrary pattern called academic English. The forms include standard written English grammar, lexical choices, a type of structure of argumentation, and even a certain form of citation, all specified and enforced by the Bergin and Garvey proofreader. These features largely match other similar texts. In a traditional analysis, that similarity would be treated as an epiphenomenon—an insignificant consequence of the fact that all the texts follow the same rules. However, looked at in terms of the informational potential of the texts, that interpretation is unlikely. What is more likely is that the similarities between this text and others make an intertextual statement of affiliation. By the same token, this text differs from some patterns that are generally followed in language-related studies, such as the singular *they*s and split infinitive in the last paragraph. Those norm violations can be seen as making a statement of difference and will no doubt irritate some readers, though they may also please others. These violations are still crucially minimized intertextually by the widespread disregard for these particular prescriptive rules in educated discourse, journalistic writing, and, increasingly, scientific texts (Newman 1997). A more drastic divergence from generic practice, say, negative concord—the prohibition of which is just as unfounded as that of split infinitives and the enforcement of pronoun-antecedent agreement— would not be successful. The intertextual connections are entirely wrong, associated as they are with vernacular forms of expression. They pull the text too far from its generic center of gravity.

The extremely oblique, abstract, and inconsistent nature of this type of information explains why the case-study students actively worked to construct models of their instructors' specific expectations. The normative nature of these models accounts for why they were often couched in terms of what might be called negative information, what writers should *not* do. For example, Will began his psychology writing class with a highly positive expectation influenced by the expressivist-oriented composition classes he had had in his community college. In his words, "I love writing classes because I can talk about my feelings and my interpretations, and then if it's completely off base, then they can tell me, and if there's something they don't agree with we can talk about it. Usually the teachers are pretty good about that."

Yet the next week, after reading the course handbook on writing, his expectations began to focus on two properly metainformational issues, norms of rhetorical organization and unbiased ways to refer to individuals and groups, both of which he couched in the negative terms of what to avoid:

> *Will*: With scientific writing, they try to keep you away from being wordy; you know about how a lot of people are with a tendency to be very detailed, and they want you to be detailed but in a simplistic way. . . . [The course handbook] I think will help me out a lot. They talk about everything from sexism to racial issues to everything that I think, you know, make it a very politically correct paper [laughs].

The week after that, however, just before handing in his first assignment, he decided that discrimination was not an issue for him. Instead, he found himself in the midst of a struggle with language based mainly, as he saw it, on the issue of tense consistency and not misusing vocabulary. In other words, Will constructed an understanding that his goal in the assignment was to avoid problems that he had received feedback on in the past. This switch was based on his interpretation of the instructor's description of his assignment on the first of seven short essays. He believed the instructor was "more interested in our writing style than our arguments"; furthermore, "Our arguments are graded, but he said he'd left it open so much that it would be easy for us."

In fact, the instructor told us that his system was one-third content, one-third structure—including organization and logic—and one-third mechanics. Whereas Will had thought of the assignment as easy, that may have been because he had trouble conceiving of generic features as subject to grading beyond mechanical errors. So he interpreted the instructor's de-emphasis of the arguments, together with the fact that the instructor was "a nice guy," as a sign of openness and ease in grading. The next week, however, he found out that he had received only sixteen points out of a possible thirty, which he claimed was above average. His construction of the problem then changed radically, though it was still couched in negative terms:

Will: Everybody is pretty much writing in the style that we've learned through our entire life, which is not very descriptive, more of like an implied meaning for a lot of things, and the scientific writing for psychology has to be very spelled out. It has to be very, you know, can't really imply much, and if you do, it has to be very, very clear; you can't have a word in there that means two different things.

Note how much conceptual growth there is between this citation and the previous one. On the level of declarative knowledge, Will shows an awareness of generic issues, although perhaps he is still too concerned with concrete facets such as lexical semantics. This citation also provides another source for the negativity of the normative task models that students construct at the same time that it adds a positive element. To be successful in this class means a modification of an old network of norms whenever they vary from the new ones expected in class. Of course, as long-time sophisticated language users, the students arrive at class with a number of models in place, and they must keep those norms that apply to the new genre as they replace the ones that do not. For example, they must replace implication with explicit description, and replace ambiguous words with unambiguous ones, at the same time that they keep standard English grammar. It can be hard to determine what has to stay and what has to go, and many babies may get tossed out with the bath water.

Not surprisingly, therefore, Will expressed confusion as to which modifications were necessary in his own writing. He did not know how to achieve the directness he knew he needed to aim for, and he changed his models weekly as each hypothesized modification failed to produce an essay that satisfied his instructor. By the seventh week he became less able to generate hypotheses about what was expected of him, and frustration set in. All he enunciated was the sheer difficulty of the course, without, however, entirely abdicating his own responsibility for his low writing grades.

Paradoxically, about this time Will received back the political science midterm with full credit on the essay portion plus comments by the TA extolling his excellent essays. While this grade boosted his self-esteem, it also left him more mystified about psychology:

Will: I've tried everything that I can think of, and I don't feel much improvement. I've gone to the writing center for my papers four times now. . . . I actually hired somebody to proofread my paper once. . . . At the beginning it was a challenge . . . OK try to do better; try to improve and after four papers and . . . I don't know. I just don't see an improvement. . . . I don't know if it is [the instructor's] fault or if it's ours or what. I'm not going to point any fingers, but I do want to talk to him about it because I'm getting more frustrated now to the point to where I'm just more angry than taking this as a challenge.

Investig.: Angry at?

Will: The fact that I can't grasp this stuff. It just doesn't seem right. I'm not saying it's his fault; maybe he can give me some ideas on how to do better. . . . Every other week I've been in there talking to him, and there just doesn't seem to be any improvement at all.

Our analysis of Will's papers indicated a number of problems on the level of register, concepts employed, and purpose. In particular, he tended to answer the questions directly, focusing on the phenomena being examined and not using them as vehicles to employ psychological concepts, something implicit in the instructor's conception of the task. His very interest in the problems, and particularly the fact that he had thought about them on a personal level, caused him to write about them from the point of view of personal experience. The result was an oral-influenced register and impressionistic rather than abstract employment of notions such as validity, means, repressed memory, math anxiety, and so on. His instructor was a doctoral student working as a teaching assistant, and although he was dedicated to his class's learning, he had no training in writing instruction. He was baffled by how to help Will, who he was quite concerned about because he was evidently trying so hard.

What ended up working for Will was an examination of Psychology Dissertation Abstracts and use of them as models, which in a departure from my role as researcher I suggested he do. This was the only intervention I actively made in students' work, and I did it mostly because my concern for Will's frustration overrode my feelings of obligation to remain a neutral observer, but also in part because I wanted to see if my emerging analysis of his failings was correct. The abstracts seemed an obvious choice to me because they contain about the same number of words as the short papers he was assigned. They also employ the same highly austere prose needed to cover fairly broad topics in such a short space, and they provide examples of the detached register that the instructor expected. On his last paper, Will received twenty-six out of thirty points—equivalent to an A−. I was pleased for him and felt vindicated in my conclusions.

In contrast to Will, Greg found success in writing too easily:

> *Greg*: I remember writing a paper and getting a really positive reaction from my professor, you know just really impressed her evidently. Now I had written this paper late at night, the night before, based on some facts from my class, but I don't think the facts or even the concepts were instrumental in the impression that she got. I think it was more the language, and it even felt like "boy, it doesn't really matter so much what you write but how you write it."

Whether Greg's reaction to this teacher's response was accurate, it created in him a conscious model of task type for writing papers that essentially individuated a set of genre norms that he had already, judging by his grades, been discriminating. Be that as it may, when I challenged him on the claim he had made that the rhetorical features involved in "academic style" were vacuous, his response was revealing.

> *Greg*: I did take a look at it from a number of sides, and I did set up scenarios where I would make an assumption, and based on the assumption critique family leave policy for working parents. Then I would make another assumption and then critique it again and another one and critique it again and then summarize all of the different critiques, and so there was something . . . that was also appealing. You know it made sense evidently, and I just got the impression that the reason that it struck such a chord was that I used fancy language, appropriately.

He nevertheless still critiqued academic language for its opacity, and felt uncomfortable with his own production of it. An example of his successful approach and what he was criticizing can be seen in the opening sentence from a paper for his Changing Family class:

The thing that strikes me most about Giddens' *The Transformation of Intimacy* is his reoccurring concept of intimacy as a progressively more liberating facet of individuality which intentionally breaks from the prior norm of intimacy as a result of commitment seen by Giddens as a restrictive promise.

Greg's comment was that this sentence was "loaded" and "not clear." Although this may be true, his sentence reaches so far beyond the generic expectations of a paper for an undergraduate course that it hardly matters. It displays personal engagement with the subject matter, confidence in the meaning extracted, critique of a reading, and employment of a number of abstract concepts. The sentence is indeed somewhat difficult to parse, but it is (unfortunately) not unlike what is found in much published academic writing.

Yet because the instructor let slip two grammar errors later in the paper, Greg suspected her of not really reading his work and giving it an A based on style alone. In fact, Greg played normative games, an example of which can be seen on the essay question discussed on page 99. These games even rose to the level of writing the letters marking his multiple-choice selections in varying sizes and outlandish shapes (Figure 6.2).

Figure 6.2
Greg's Wild Multiple-Choice Letters

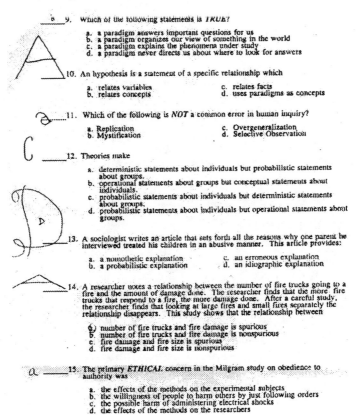

It should be remembered that Greg was not entirely successful in fulfilling metainformational expectations. As we saw in the discussion of structural aspects of concepts, he got into trouble for violating Professor Tomko's conception of a major norm of pedagogical genres, the presentation of definitions of the concepts being assessed. It should be noted that Professor Tomko justified her requirement for detailed specific information on other metainformational grounds. These can be seen in response to my challenge that she would not include structural aspects of concepts in her own sociology articles:

Tomko: Would I say that? I think that I would want to know if I'm describing the descriptive statistics. I'd want to say the descriptive statistics tell me that the people in this sample read an average of five newspapers. I wouldn't want them to say the mean is five. Sometimes you will just say the mean is five, but I think it is much better style, and this is the thing I try to encourage in my students is to talk in these terms.

Metainformational issues affected reception as well as creation of writing. The simplest cases involved test questions, which Sophie had the most problems with. Painfully aware of her difficulties, she panicked when faced with practice questions (taken from an old exam) that took forms she was not familiar with, and she rushed to her Chemistry TA in tears. She only felt better after the TA worked through the questions with her and she became able to parse them on her own. At times, she also used metainformational strategies to decide on choices on tests when she was unable to determine the answer by other means. One such strategy could be called an informational distance strategy: "Do not pick any choice if it seems the same as another choice." Other metainformational strategies she used included:

- selecting the longest choice.
- matching words between choice and item stem.
- picking choices containing unknown words.

Obviously, these methods have varying degrees of success, but test writers should consider them as ways that some students approach these types of assessments. Evidently, if the longest choice is consistently the target, students can achieve a high score for the wrong reasons. Sophie's testing travails were not limited to multiple-choice formats. She could easily be confused in short answers as well as by what was expected, a factor examined in more detail in the Chapter 7.

Unlike Will, however, she had developed a certain fatalism regarding her inability to figure out how to deal with the various types of test questions. Whereas Will made every effort to improve and blamed himself for his failures, Sophie seemed to believe she would never improve and resigned herself to mediocre grades. As she saw it, she was "a C student," as if this were an immutable quality.

SUMMARY

The six types of information described in this chapter include facts, connections, concepts, processes, principles, and metainformation. They constitute the substance of the information recycling game as it was realized by these four students in the various classes that they took. They are the different elements that make up course content and assessments. The two better students had a greater appreciation of the differences between the types of information and how they could be used. The less successful ones were frequently at a loss to explain or see these differences.

Different researchers in the area of epistemics (e.g., Langer 1992, Hammer 1994; Alexander and Dochy 1994; Schommer 1994) have pointed out the importance of students going beyond learning knowledge as isolated bits of information, what I am calling facts. Their findings are paralleled here by the findings of how the case-study students working with more abstract forms of information yields better grades. Yet unlike these authors, I have deliberately avoided entering issues of learning and assumed an informational rather than a cognitive stance. That stance, I believe, yields the more fine-grained depiction presented here.

Furthermore, the hypothesis put forward here is that a deeper appreciation of the different types of information and the properties of each type allows students greater control over content. It would follow that enlightening students on how the types of information differ and their various properties would promote greater success. This kind of curriculum would go beyond the kind of general prescriptions to connect information or engage in critical thinking that arises from the epistemic literature. It asks students to become aware of the different types of information they find in their course content, of the informational expectations on exams, and of the different properties of the information they interact with. Of course, determining the usefulness of such an approach could only be the result of a study very different from the present effort, one involving curriculum development and testing.

NOTES

1. Situations by definition can be broken down in this way. The idea is similar to how a chair can be thought of as its component features. This is the case when, for example, we need to discuss a crack in the seat or at least need to consider that as a possibility.

2. The asterisk indicates ungrammaticality, as is customary in linguistics.

3. I ignore the prescriptive issue of the singular *they* because such usages commonly appear in speech and print (Newman 1997).

4. *Distractor* and *target* are the technical terms for what are more prosaically called *a wrong answer* and *right answer*, respectively.

5. It should be noted that Weinstein and Meyer themselves emphasize the use of elaboration strategies not so much for schema structuring but rather for the linking of new with old knowledge, a more traditional view of the use of schema theory.

6. They will be treated as concepts in a later section.

7. The fourth logically possible perspective, a structural view of a simple concept, is not really conceptual because in such a case the concept is being treated as a fact.

8. The concept is the way bases (e.g., lye) combine with lipids (e.g., grease or oil) to make soap and detergent. Therefore, adding a milder, and so safer, base such as ammonia to oil in a stain will also create a kind of soap-like substance, which then washes out. I pass on this application for the benefit of those readers who may find themselves in need of it. However, Sophie never felt the class was any use to her. I myself must admit inconsistent results.

9. Tecumseh is the pseudonym I have given to MSU's hometown.

10. Note that *processes* here refers to only those that students actually perform, not ones they learn about such as chemical reactions, political developments, and so on.

Chapter 7

Operations on Information

The previous chapter described in detail how the students who participated in this research categorized the material they were working with. They were not entirely aware of these categorizations. They did not even always individuate all of them, but they at least clearly discriminated the types of information that, in effect, constitute a typology of the material used in the achievement game, analogous to classes of chess pieces or the different suits and ranks of cards. In this chapter, I describe what they did with course content—the moves they made or the hands they played.

The term I use to describe these moves, *operations*, is taken from arithmetic, where it refers to actions on numbers such as addition, subtraction, multiplication, and division. It is intended to capture a similar sense of single actions on abstract entities that can be combined and ordered in different ways to accomplish useful tasks. There are four informational operations, just as there are four arithmetic ones. However, here the similarities end because the four informational operations I propose—*exposure, extraction, manipulation*, and *display*—are not logically related to each other as arithmetic ones are. No operation is the opposite of another as addition and subtraction or multiplication and division are; nor is one based on iterations of another as multiplication is of addition. Also, I make no claims for the type of universality that characterizes arithmetic operations, although it is certainly possible that they may turn out to have broader application beyond academic communication.

Still, the atomic nature of operations distinguishes them from study-strategy taxonomies such as Weinstein and Meyer's (1991) repetition, elaboration, and organization types. The potential for confusion is present if only because each strategy corresponds to a particular cognitive objective. So repetition strategies are used for memorization, elaboration strategies to link new information to prior knowledge, and organization strategies to create new knowledge. Also, Weinstein and Meyer include specific activities as examples of strategies. So they consider underlining, for instance, to be a "repetition strategy," summarizing an "elaboration strategy," and outlining an "organization strategy."

Despite the intuitive attractiveness and usefulness of these categories—and I have made use of them earlier in this study to illustrate various points—there are some problems that limit their descriptive capacity. For instance—to anticipate some findings to be detailed later—Sophie and Will appeared to use outlining in ways that did not correspond to the organization-type purposes Weinstein and Meyer assign to it. Surprisingly, they reported that outlining did not change the way they thought about content, as an organization strategy must do by definition. Instead, they saw it as a way of reinforcing memory, a purpose Weinstein and Meyer would assign to a repetition strategy. Greg, by contrast, largely did find that outlining transformed his understanding by creating new connections. This divergence puts into doubt the one-to-one correspondence of activity with cognitive goal.

Although this weakness might be repaired by declaring some uses of outlining to be repetition or to find that Will and Sophie did not use outlining correctly, there are deeper flaws in the taxonomy. One can be seen by the consideration of underlining or highlighting as a strategy of any kind. To do so confuses the act of underlining or highlighting with what is really a longer routine of reviewing a segment of material. It is the whole routine, not the act of highlighting, that merits being considered a strategy of learning by rehearsing or repeating. Furthermore, although the research participants often used highlighting as the first step of the memorization-by-review routine, they did not always do so. Carmin sometimes used it as the first step in a much more elaborate strategy when she fed the highlighted information into a mental visualization activity. Other times, she marked off sections of text for further clarification because she either had not understood that part or at least felt that she had missed certain implications on a first reading. Will highlighted almost exclusively when he did not understand rather than use this activity for memorization. Greg signaled central concepts and nexuses in connections by highlighting them, thus implicitly marking relations. What highlighting did in all these cases was to remove some text, and therefore the information it contained,

from the mass of other material and so *extracted* it for any number of
purposes. Furthermore, it was not so much a strategy to extract but a
way of extracting. To consider it a strategy would be like describing
sequentially lifting one leg after another and moving one leg after
another forward and up as a strategy for climbing stairs; it vacates
the notion of almost all its sense of planning and calculation.

To return to the case of outlining, using the same, more formal approach helps explain why there was a divergence of effects among the
respondents. Greg's outlines changed the way he understood the material because he created them from what he was reading in his notes
and books. He found implicit hierarchical connections and made them
explicit. Sophie and Will by contrast limited themselves to copying
the hierarchical structures they found in textbook chapter and section headings and teacher-provided materials, as recommended by
study-skills manuals. They noticed and copied these hierarchical
relations rather than developed them in their own minds. It is Greg's
kind of act of creation of new information, not making an outline
(which again is several possibly different steps), that allows one to
say that an organization-type purpose is being fulfilled.

In contrast to *strategies*, the idea of *operation* is designed to look
at each of the students' study activities on its own without prejudg-
ing its ultimate purpose, so it does not confuse the immediate effect with that purpose. Just as there are many reasons to move a
rook in chess, so it is that there are many possible reasons to highlight, outline, or talk to a friend about a lecture. Finally, it is worth
considering the big picture so that we do not lose sight of the forest
in our close-up of the trees. Each operation is used by students to
determine and locate the course content in whatever sources it can
be found in and advance it toward a display on some assessment
for points. In sum, the proposed taxonomy of operations provides a
cleaner and simpler system for describing how students manage
course content for grades in classes. All four operations are sum-
marized in Table 7.1. The farther right the processes are in Table 7.1,
the more they imply an active, creative role for the student. At the
same time, information tends to flow from operations on the left to
those on the right. For example, a student might hear any combination of the six types of information in a lecture and/or read about
them in a book (*exposure*). Then that student might take selective
notes or highlight the relevant sections of text containing some of
this information (*extraction*). After that, he or she could engage in
a visualization of the material connecting, say, different facts or
concepts in one schema (*manipulation*). Finally, the student could
write a text that reveals implicitly or explicitly those connections
or concepts on an exam or in a paper (*display*).

Table 7.1
Information Operations

	exposure	extraction	manipulation	display
Description	Students brought information to consciousness.	Students found and isolated information from the mass of other materials.	Students used information to synthesize new information.	Students exhibited information.
Examples	Listening in a lecture, noticing while reading assignments or reviewing texts.	Deciding what to include in notes, highlighting, or making flashcards.	Efforts to comprehend texts, visualizing relationships, thinking about readings or lectures.	Writing papers, notes, answering oral or exercise questions, making oral presentations, taking tests.

In reality, the ordering of operations was usually far more complex, and the case-study students would often perform various ones in tandem, as Greg did when he outlined directly from a reading. In this case, he was simultaneously using all four operations; he was exposing himself to information while extracting, manipulating, and displaying some of it on a piece of paper. Similarly, the ordering was not always that indicated by going left to right in Table 7.1. The case-study students sometimes began by making considerable effort to make sense out of a difficult reading (*manipulation*) or highlighting confusing portions of one, as we have seen (*extraction*). Also, displays were sometimes performed as a self-test or with a classmate, TA, or professor in a nonassessment setting for practice. This was the purpose of chapter and section learning checks in textbooks. Furthermore, these often also provoked manipulation, extraction, and exposure since the students needed to look for and alter content—to figure something out—to create the display. Finally, lecture notes themselves consist of displays of information.

The following annotated description by Greg of preparing for his Methods midterm illustrates how the operations could be ordered and reiterated. Each mention of an operation is enclosed in curly brackets {}, and the specific operation is indicated in a subscript following the closing bracket:

Greg: {I paid attention in class}$_{\text{exposure}}$ and {had often purposefully tried to construct that overarching perspective, "Where do all of these things fit in that he's talking about?" I would ask myself, "Uh, where's this going? How would this method look if I were doing it in the field?"}$_{\text{manipulation}}$ and {I imagined typing up the survey}$_{\text{manipulation}}$ {while he's talking about question formation on a survey.}$_{\text{exposure}}$ {I didn't take notes}$_{\text{extraction}}$ most of the time while I was doing that; however, it was very good for the exam {to talk with [a classmate] for about two hours}$_{\text{manipulation/display}}$ {about things he mentioned in class.}$_{\text{extraction}}$ It was a time for me {to vocalize things}$_{\text{display}}$ that {I had until then just accepted aurally just by sitting in class}$_{\text{exposure}}$ and {put them into my own words.}$_{\text{manipulation/display}}$

Therefore, while actual studying activities takes various forms, these students' efforts could always be broken down *conceptually* into differing combinations of these four categories of operations. Such an analysis provides, I would argue, the most precise language available for discussing the Design of what students are doing with course content in their classes. It allows comparisons across students and courses that are not possible without this kind of formalization.

In the rest of the chapter, I will describe each operation in more detail and reveal some glaring differences between students in how and when they employed them and the consequences their various approaches had on the information they moved from source to target.

EXPOSURE

Exposure consists of an effort to bring elements of course content to consciousness, to make oneself aware of information. To do so, the students in this study variously read, reviewed, paid attention to lectures and recitations, replayed and transcribed recorded lectures, and listened to classmates. Listeners and readers can become aware of any of the six types of information, as long as the words or diagrams simply bring them to mind.

It could be argued that the encounters with information are really cognitively more active than this description implies, particularly for the more abstract forms of information. However, when an experienced reader or listener understands the overarching schema, these active processes can be highly automatic. Without getting into issues better left to cognitive science, there is certainly a substantial difference between how individuals approach easy or familiar content and how they approach more difficult or novel course information.

Although facts would seem to be the easiest form of information to think of, concepts, connections, principles, and metainformational features can also come effortlessly into awareness when the requisite schemas are already in place. Under the right circumstances, a person can recognize instantaneously a Marxist analysis, a usage of jargon, or the reason why a t-test is appropriate. The information is experienced as just appearing to come into consciousness (Wittgenstein 1953, pp. 193–214).[1] Therefore, because my focus is on the individual's *intention and interaction* instead of underlying cognitive processes, it seems reasonable to consider it *exposure* if only to differentiate this form of interaction from those requiring conscious effort.

The participants used exposure in two broad contexts: (1) when encountering new information and (2) when reviewing previously seen information. Both involve an identical action—a drawing to awareness—and the division between them is admittedly somewhat artificial because, for example, a reader is likely to notice new content on a second reading of a text. Yet there were differences that resulted from the context of use. For example, Greg and Carmin tended to combine initial exposure with manipulation, while Will and Sophie did not. Also, Greg and Carmin tended to use reexposure sparingly compared with Sophie and Will, whose studying consisted mostly of multiple return visits to various texts, particularly class notes. Their overreliance on exposure appeared, in turn, to obey a mistaken belief that learning, or at least memorization, was best accomplished through this operation. As Will put it, "The only way I'm gonna have to really get a hold of this information is just to keep going over it."

Reliance on exposure reflected, in Will's case, what might be called a photographic theory of memory, according to which the picturing of an item of information in consciousness leads to remembering it. If memory is like photography, the longer the exposure one has or the more repetitions one makes, the more deeply engraved the image would be. Given that view, it is hardly surprising that it never occurred to Will to test out his learning by some form of display beyond notes, say, talking it over with someone else. Nor did he use the information as a building block to construct something else (i.e., manipulation), unless he was instigated to by the instructor or task. He largely used manipulation to become aware of information he did not understand, to bring it into focus so to speak.

Will's understanding of student as camera clashed, interestingly enough, with the advice given in the study-skills books that he had read and even with what he was learning about memory in his psychology classes. These sources described, in their different ways, an active engagement with information as crucial to learning. Faced with this contradiction, Will made some minimal modifications to his belief system and arrived at the ingeniously misleading conclusion that rewriting constituted active engagement. He then convinced himself, despite the evidence to the contrary in the form of

his continuing mediocre test scores, that this copying helped him.
That was the reason he gave for transcribing his lectures and rewriting his notes in the two classes he was doing poorly in, Psychology Writing and Biology.

Although I can only speculate about this, I suspect that Will's
resistance to changing his photographic theory of learning was related to the fact that it was only one part of an overall epistemic
system. If I am right, it would be associated with his fact-centered
perspective discussed in the previous chapter. As I said, while it is
possible to envision a connection or concept without conscious mental effort, it is less clear that it is possible to develop a new one that
way. Novel abstract information appears to require a more constructivist approach, if only because those forms of information can
often not be explicitly stated but must be inferred and expressed
indirectly. Even when grasped as a whole, as Wittgenstein (1953,
§422–427) notes, pictures of concepts and connections can be tricky
and misleading. In fact, Wittgenstein uses the untrustworthiness
of conceptual pictures as a major argument for the pragmatic view
of understanding that characterizes his philosophy. He argues, in
the end, that understanding is the ability to *do* something, or as he
puts it, "to go on" rather than as a purely mental process accessible
to consciousness (Wittgenstein 1953, §153–155).

Exploring why Sophie also tended to rely on reexposure was hard
because she had great difficulty in explicating her reading and study
processes. When first asked how she read, she replied, "I just read,"
not really understanding the point of the question. Pressed, she
sounded a bit like Will: "No highlighting, no taking notes. I feel
like it takes my attention away from what I'm reading and trying
to understand." The key word here is "attention." Sophie was also
relying on exposure. Based on her logs and her comments on her
actual readings, it seemed that to Sophie manipulation was not
absent; it was just not employed well or consistently. Finally, we
concluded that she believed that reading should be a function of
rudimentary metacognition. Her goal in reading was to arrive at a
feeling of understanding, much like it was for Will. This sense of
closure would permit her to go on; lack of it should lead to manipulating, although she said she was sometimes "too lazy" to do that.
The difference with Will was that she was somewhat more aware
that getting the facts into the picture was not enough, and she felt
she should look to see how it all made sense.

As the "too lazy" self-criticism indicates, even this impressionistic criterion was not always reached, and the problem here lay in
motivation: the less she liked the material, the less intensively she

would read it. For this reason, she only skimmed much of her Political Science readings about Mexico in front of the television before giving up entirely. She claimed that the television had no deleterious effects on her studying. Nevertheless, she also said she would pay more attention if she actually cared about the subject matter, as she had in her previous Sociology courses and would again, she assured us, in her future social work ones. Political Science and Chemistry by contrast were, as I mentioned in Chapter 4, just hoops to jump through, inconsiderately placed in her path by the administration of MSU. She was not going to collaborate by actually making enough effort to learn the material or even just to get an A. She indeed was less careful than Will and often just read and reread the same passage or notes over and over again. The only intensive reviews she made were with her flash cards of chemical formulas, and note that these are still exposure-based, requiring little mental creativity.

In this way, it is easy to see how Greg and Carmin's more supple and complex sequences of operations relate directly to the types of information they were interested in. The two more successful students were looking more at concepts and connections and, in some cases, principles; so they were altering information they were initially exposed to. Simple repetition, by contrast, tends to highlight new facts and already familiar conceptual content. Looked at in terms of Entwistle's (1984, 1987) taxonomy, studying centered around exposure is the paradigmatic case of a surface approach. This kind of studying unifies all the various characteristics of this approach given by Entwistle, including limitation to task requirements, memorization, conflation of principles and examples, a view of tasks as impositions, a focus on discrete bits of information, and a lack of reflection.

For Greg and Carmin, by contrast, reexposure was most often just a brief review of notes and highlighted portions as kind of a jogging of memory just before an exam. The material reviewed had already been subject to extraction, manipulation, and often display. As a result, these participants were reexperiencing the information in a context somewhat different from that in which they had first seen it, because they now had a more fully developed understanding of related information. They would also sometimes reexpose themselves to information by reading sections in books related to the lecture or looking over highlighted portions of the text in the middle of studying. But note that these activities also change the perspective somewhat. If there is an image still being photographed, it is viewed from a different angle.

EXTRACTION

Extraction consists of selecting information from the larger mass of content available in a course. It is an act of choosing, a kind of triage in which students decide that certain content merits special attention or treatment for some reason. Obviously, an ability to select the information that will ultimately be expected on an exam or paper and to discard the rest is quite useful for a student. It means not having to waste time and energy on content that will not gain points. Greg and Carmin were not only more accurate in their selection than Sophie and Will, but they also were more selective generally and so eliminated more information from consideration. Also, they did so much earlier in the process than their two weaker counterparts.

The two more successful students mostly used two often overlapping criteria to decide what was likely to score maximum points on an exam. The first was whether the information could be identified as inherently important, either as a useful concept or central nexus in a web of connections. Had Carmin identified Delphi as a key location, she would have gotten the TA's question on which oracle predicted Oedipus's fate correctly. On the other hand, she did consistently identify all the major components of theories of human development. Greg's comment, quoted in full in Chapter 5, that "It's usually not that hard to guess what's gonna be on the exam. You go through the chapters; you pick out the main topics of each chapter; and you don't go into the details" is an example of this kind of reasoning.

The second criterion was whether there were direct hints by the instructor that some information might lead to points on an exam or paper. Such hints could consist of an emphasis made by the professor or TA in class or because there was some other reason to believe that the instructor was more likely to put one question rather than another on an exam. Greg's determination that the Russian Revolution would appear on the final based on the fact that it was the topic of the History professor's dissertation is a particularly clever employment of this strategy. It gets at an instructor's idiosyncratic predilections the way that a clever chess player can use knowledge of an opponent's personality or style to anticipate their moves in a given situation on the board. Carmin realized that despite the fact that it was hardly relevant to issues of social policy, she had to memorize the seven definitions of "reality" given to her in that class because it appeared to be important to the professor. Another successful student I interviewed aptly referred to this kind of maneuver as "reading the teacher."[2]

Whichever of the two criteria they used, the same principle held; Greg and Carmin actively determined what to extract by working backward from their projected exams and papers. So they determined what content would be needed and what could be discarded based on what they thought would yield a maximum number of points. Will, by contrast, for most of the quarter had a particularly poorly developed understanding of extraction, one that did not really take the exam into account. He constructed the process of determining useful information as separating "important things" from "filler . . . stuff that you have to cut through." It was as if he believed that textbooks and lectures were far longer than they needed to be, much the way that useful ore was found embedded in useless rock. In particular, note the contrast with Greg's description of some parts as simply too peripheral to appear on an exam, which at least leaves them as part of the same conceptual schema. It is not surprising therefore that Will was so uncertain about what needed to be extracted that he put this process off as long as he could. One reason that he recorded his lectures was that he was afraid to leave anything important out. Similarly, he felt that concentrating while reading—crucial given his photographic theory of learning—was incompatible with highlighting, which he said "only puts off learning." The idea was to remember it as he read it the first time around and to remember it all.

Fortunately, this belief system was not static. In any case, by the fifth week he had abandoned the idea of "learning it as he read it" as probably not workable, and by the end of the quarter, he had improved at his extraction and had begun to successfully work backward from the assessment task. On the psychology final, he was pleased to note that he had "anticipated a lot of the questions, and I got a lot of them right. You know, I figured, 'OK that's gonna be on there.'" His guesses were based on a greater understanding of the material generally, and although he was still taking too long to reach that point, he was beginning to think strategically.

As I write this, I imagine some readers responding with dismay to the calculated nature of this entire process of eliminating from consideration content that we would like students to engage with. In fact, faculty appear have an ambivalent, if not contradictory, response to students' strategic approaches to extraction. On the one hand, most of the ones we interviewed expressed a frustration with questions of the type, "Will this be covered on the exam?" On the other hand, they still aided the process. The most common way was to emphasize points, repeat them over and over again, or simply directly tell students that they were important or would be on an exam. Professor Haus's outlines could be seen in this light as

well. Reading materials also aided extraction by textual enhancements (e.g., bold-facing), use of headings, or use of graphics. Of
course, such assistance can be understood in terms of learning as
well as the achievement game. After all, they can be simply considered as helping students determine what information was inherently more important.

Yet faculty do not get off so easily. They also used other aids to
extraction that were less easily justified in terms of learning. For
example, the Biology and Statistics professors provided study guides
a week before their exams. Professor Thomas made old exams available to students in the Chemistry recitation sessions before both
midterm and final exams. The most extreme form of this kind of
scaffolding of extraction was to provide a set of questions from which
the actual final would be chosen, as Greg's History and Carmin's
Policy professors did. Doing so allows students to disregard wide
swaths of content and focus on particular points within those areas
covered when cramming. It is thus somewhat disingenuous for faculty not to acknowledge our role in the game and claim that we are
only interested in learning. In the end, our actions resemble nothing so much as what are called "nonplaying characters" in role-
playing games, such as the dungeon master in Dungeons and
Dragons. Like these characters, our function is to guide the actions
of players but not to compete (Newman 2001).

A third reason to extract information was when some point was
only partly understood or not understood at all. Will and Carmin
both at some point highlighted sections to be reread later. Similarly, Will talked about isolating information that he was not sure
he had learned, even if he felt he understood it. "I might've highlighted this because I wasn't sure that I had gotten it into my mind,"
he said when I questioned him as to why he was violating his "no
highlighting" policy. More generally, he said, "When I go back
through [a reading] . . . I'll still go back to specific parts. I mean I'll
usually go through like three or four times to make sure that there's
no questions that I have."

MANIPULATION

Manipulation consists of using one form of information to reveal
or synthesize another. It involves the creation of knowledge. A professor never needs to state connections or to define or apply concepts explicitly to expect a student to deduce them from a set of
facts given. In fact, it is often not effective communication to directly state concepts and connections, for reasons discussed in Chapter 6, but it is better to show rather than to tell. Similarly, the

meaning of a text may not be apparent to a reader who does not have sufficient background or familiarity with vocabulary or discourse structure assumed by the author. The reader has to do a lot of work to make even initial sense of it. Finally, sometimes facts and connections fall out naturally from uses of concepts, so teachers do not have to explicitly discuss them for students to be expected to produce them on demand. Even in this case, thought is required because the student must know to think through consequences or deduce applications.

For students this means that college can be something like a mystery novel full of red herrings in which the clues can be easily missed, and there were, not surprisingly, significant differences between the stronger and weaker students in this area. However, even the lower-achieving students were at least tacitly aware that working their way around a confusing informational environment was an integral part of their academic experience. It was an expected if not always welcome challenge. They differed only in what they thought clues would look like and how agile and, above all, independent they were at using them.

One expression of agility is the time at which manipulation began. Greg and Carmin began to manipulate as soon as they were initially exposed to information in class or a reading. They proactively and automatically tended to manipulate the information they encountered in real time. Look, for example, at Figure 7.1, which is a page of Greg's notes from the Changing Family class. Greg often took notes with a pen and highlighter in hand. The highlighted portions—which appear as boxed text in the figure—are more central points, so indicated after being written down. Furthermore, each thought is related to others either implicitly or with graphic indications such as textual enhancements, bullets, or lines. There are even questions at the end that represent Greg's responses to the content delivered. It is important to note that this pattern did not depend on the teacher making or not making connections in class. Greg's lecture notes all have this pattern, whatever the class, and in the next chapter I will provide a similar example from Greg's History class, which is interesting because of Greg's complaints that the instructor did not do her part in connecting information.

Greg also manipulated while reading. In the following example, he describes one of his favorite ways of doing so: mental visualizations:

Greg: When I picked up *Ivan Denisovich* at the library this week and flipped through the pages, all I had to do was read one sentence or two sentences and an image came up in my mind of the book when I read. It's very much like I create my own movie in my head. I see things. I

Figure 7.1
Greg's Changing Family Notes

1 in 5 Kids live in poverty. [20% Kids are poor]
one factor is 'non-custodial' parents. Absent parents

Small change: The Economics of Childsupport

chance of BEING AWARDED CHILD SUPPORT increased 1978-85
(BUT   AV AMOUNT DECLINED.
Most policies have little effect on child support payments

_____

60% of ♀ AWARDED SUPPORT
        only 80% RECEIVED part of IT   20% DIDN'T
        only 50% RECEIVED ALL of IT.

Visiting fathers more likely to make payments.

The type of household w/ lowest median income is Female
                                                  Headed
                                                  ($7,000)

Consequences of Divorce on Children
  - school BEHAVIOR · ACHIEVEMENT suffers
  - more likely to be delinquent
  - young ♀ more likely to become single mothers themselves.
  - [younger kids] more seriously [disadvantaged]
  - boys seen more harmed by disruption (?)
            BUT HOW MUCH? SIGNIFICANTLY?
            ONLY SHORT TERM or LONGTERM?
            DUE TO DIVORCE or SINGLEPARENT?
                           itself

create the landscape. I have a mental image of how that concentration camp would look like, and that's how I remember things.

Again, Greg adds to the content of the incoming information, this time with a setting in which it takes place. In his later studying, he took this same visual/narrative strategy to astonishing lengths, and his use of images was not limited to fiction but applied to any series of events that could take on a narrative format. The extensive excerpt on p. 81 was an example of how it applied to the concrete task of remembering events of the Russian Revolution using a combination of the textbook and his notes as he crammed for the final.

What the visualization did was largely to create connections between the different events and those events and kind of stock situations, like the Germans sending Lenin off to Russia. Greg's visualization of connections was not limited to narratives but was also used for descriptions of an event itself:

Investig.: How do the [mental] pictures work? You can't picture words, you only . . .

Greg: No, I can! I can picture words and know where they are on a page like I said, but I also try to picture what those words mean. For example, when they were talking about the Congress of Vienna, I, in my mind, imagined Vienna. I was lucky enough to have been there one time. I didn't go to the place where they had the Congress, but I tried to imagine that area and people coming up in horses and carriages and walking off and going into a building and all of these people standing around thinking, "Gee, who are those guys?" and not realizing that it's going to be in a history book someday. And, you know, just thinking like how they acted at the table when they were talking. Like I saw a picture of [incomprehensible,] and I was thinking, "You know, did he really look like that?" And I wonder what his mannerisms were like. Trying to make what I'm reading real in the sense of history. I can do that because there they were, real people, and I oftentimes try to get past the ideal image that's presented there. You know, Napoleon does not look like he did in the picture of him going across the Alps or something, but trying to make it a little bit more accessible, and that meant making it close to the human experience that I experienced too.

With such sophisticated manipulations, Greg could even compensate late in the game for a course he had been "blowing off" by looking for the significant connections apparent in the little material he had examined. Besides visualizations of series of events, as in his cram for the final, he could also organize facts around central concepts. For example, he describes the results of his cramming for a History midterm that revolved around the concept of transformation of the state:

Greg: I'll see if I can still remember from this morning. Uh [Napoleon] transformed economics by introducing the Bank of France, transformed religion by making a deal in 1801 with Pope Pius. He transformed—now I'm gonna take some more time to think about these last two because they aren't sticking out (pause)—the legal status with the civil code. Now it's coming back to me, and the fourth one was—I arranged them into categories to help me remember, they go along with my political, economic, and the governmental's the last one—he made it a centralized government, a bureaucracy. Now that's basically a memorization game right there. I don't know that material. I understand the implications of memorizing it. I mean I understand the implication of that knowledge that I have memorized.

Investig.: What is the implication?

Greg: I get an idea of how the government changed, which is some type of knowledge.

Carmin also tended to read and develop visual images as a study technique that elaborated on the information present to anchor it into memory. However, she was a bit less creative and more mnemonic in her way of doing that than Greg was, and so it seems she was doing as much exposure as manipulation as she visualized:

Carmin: My roommates always make fun of me 'cause I stare blank into the air. They think I'm totally going through a lapse or something. [laughs]

Investig.: [laughs] That's funny. When you do this? Is this like you're looking at the definition, so you're not testing yourself essentially? You're just doing this visualization as an exercise.

Carmin: It is kind of testing myself, like I look at the word, and then I look away, and in my head I'm envisioning the definition. I can see the word, and then I know that I know it.

Investig.: OK so you are actually seeing the words passing in front of your . . .

Carmin: Uh huh.

Investig.: When did you develop this?

Carmin: I like feel, like, everything, I'm very visual oriented though. I know for geography, if we'd take map tests, I'd just look away and I could just see the map in front of me so I'd know where to put everything.

Will associated manipulation with the capture of concepts. His manipulations, however, were usually somewhat primitive, consisting of on-line rephrasing during lectures. He usually did not think of it in terms of altering the information but as an alteration of the language when not just copying verbatim. His description below shows how focused he was on not missing anything and only altering words, not information, in his processing of information:

Will: Sometimes, I'll get the concept down, but when I'm trying to think of a better way to phrase it because you know [the professor] can give a very long concept, and I'll think, "OK, how can I say this in two sentences?"

Interestingly enough, Will recognized his limitations insofar as developing concepts out of other information. He said, "I can get a concept if they give me an outline of a concept." Without such an outline he knew he might get lost. He hewed so closely to this support that his ways of organizing concepts and connections devolved into extraction rather than manipulation. Note how his lecture notes, shown in Figure 7.2, differ only in wording, and even here only occasionally, from the language provided on Professor Haus's transparency, shown in Figure 7.3. Not even the professor's outline can compare with the depth of detail and richness of connections shown in Greg's Changing Family notes in Figure 7.1.

This pattern suggested to me at first that Will had difficulties with how to manipulate information. However, I was forced to revise my view because he once described a quite sophisticated visu-

Figure 7.2
Will's Notes on "Power as an Asset"

Both an Asset (an end, goal) that you want to aquire / maintain, and a tool (a means) that you use.

one characterististic of International system is effort of States to preserve or expand their power, because system emphasize sovereign interests + self -help.

power creates insecurity.

power creates temptation

- power is expensive

- Paul Kennedy's imperial overreach summarizes military over expansion resource commitment.

Nye believes U.S. will remain leading power.

Decline of Power can be caused by rapid ↑ of non military public spending alization that appeared to be identical to the visualizations used by Greg:

Will: I wouldn't imagine myself in a delivery room or inside the placenta of an embryo or anything like that, I would just, could see like the cleavage stage, OK it's starting to break.

Investig.: A visualization?

Will: Yeah, kinda like OK I can see that. The cleavage, OK it's forming into different balls. Then it goes on the [unclear] or whatever and OK it's floating up in there, and then it goes into the blastula stage and that's where it's a hollow ball, and that's about after six days. OK, I can see that, and then OK from there it develops the endoderm, the exoderm, and the mesoderm, and I can kinda see how everything's kinda fitting into that so . . .

Investig.: So you actually sorta see the images in your head?

Will: Uh hum.

Investig.: You don't see the words or anything?

Will: Not as much, I kinda put the words maybe over it or around it, or I tie it in with maybe a visualization, but it's mostly OK, placenta, OK placenta is as I write it down. If I could imagine that, what would that be? I wouldn't have to actually see a picture of it.

Figure 7.3
Professor Haus's Transparency

Power as an Asset

- **Power is both an asset (an end, goal) that you try to acquire/maintain and a tool (a means) that you use**

- **One characteristic of international system is effort of states to preserve or expand their power because system emphsizes sovereign interests and self-help**

- **Power increases insecurity**

- **Power increases temptation**

- **Power is expensive**

- **Paul Kennedy's 'imperial overreach' summarizes military overexpansion and resource commtment**

- **Nye believes U.S. will remain leading power**

- **Decline of power can be caused by rapid expansion of nonmilitary public spending (Gilpin)**

In this way, he strengthened the connections between stages of the process of embryo development. The key thus *did not appear to lie in his inability to* manipulate so much as *his lack of understanding of the usefulness of doing so.*

Professor Haus largely arranged his class in such a way that students like Will could succeed. He had what he considered "a realistic" view of undergraduate students' abilities, and he made great efforts to provide ample scaffolding in addition to the lecture outlines. He explicitly told his students, for example, to think about the consequences of concepts such as nuclear utilization theory. He walked them through various conceptual schemata in detail, both in the outlines and in class.

By contrast, in Biology, students were supplied with large numbers of facts with few explicit pointers showing how these facts connected with each other or what the organizing concepts were. They were largely left with the hierarchical ordering of the textbook into chapters, sections, and subsections. Apart from that, the conceptual organization had to be deduced, which turned out to function as an effective, if somewhat ruthless, filtering tool for an oversubscribed major—and eventually, arguably, the health professions.

This was a serious problem for Will because, initially at least, he would usually only manipulate when he was instigated to by an assignment, say a study guide or pretest that asked provocative questions or a chapter learning check. Instead, he occasionally used mnemonics of dubious value such as picturing himself "sitting in my room and looking at that specific word when I was studying it." Fortunately, as I have noted in reference to other aspects of his academic literacy, Will showed considerable development over the quarter in his handling of manipulation as well. During the follow-up interview the next quarter, he remarked how the interview sessions had made him reflect on what he was doing. That new quarter he felt more confident, and one aspect of his confidence was an increase in the amount of manipulation and bringing in manipulation at an earlier stage in the study process:

Will: What it was [in the past], I would remember thereabouts each definition but not exactly what it meant. The more that I'm reading now, the more I'm understanding it and I can actually code it into my memory and say OK well this happens so this will happen, and since this happens this will happen. Or for logic, it will be OK this is the truth set for the "and" sign, so I can say true and everything else is false. So it's just kinda like if I get that into my memory now, I hope that at the end of the quarter I won't have to try to frantically go through every little thing and have to look everything up again. I can hopefully just go through my notes and say OK, this is this, I remember this; it's in my memory.

It should be noted that besides assigning learning checks, faculty and textbook writers elicited manipulation—perhaps more often than they scaffolded it—by combining it with display on tasks such as answering study questions and problem sets. Realizations that they had produced incorrect displays as well as the very act of constructing the display forced the students to synthesize new information from that given. Almost all of Sophie's, Will's and Carmin's manipulations took place through various forms of these practice displays.

Carmin, however, had little need for exercises, projects, and learning checks, except in the one course where she miscalculated and spent the least time, Theatre. It was thus rare for her to show a particularly proactive approach to manipulation in studying. The one case where she did was at the beginning of her quantitative methods class:

Investig.: [reading from log] "Had to read a couple of sections more than once. Also worked through LCs"

Carmin: Uhm "learning checks" the problems at the end, and that was just checking three; here I found a really hard time [laughs] obviously. [taking out exercise and pointing]

Investig.: Big question marks in pink.

Carmin: And I went to my roomate who had been in quantitative analysis, and had her go over it with me after I read it a couple of times and didn't understand it, though I've reached an understanding of it now.

Her need to use this kind of "life line" indicates the kind of limiting case of manipulation when the student just does not understand. Will went practically every week to his Psychology Writing teacher, who also provided students with a chance to write down questions and e-mail them to him for discussion in the following class. Greg had Statistics and Methods study sessions with his friend Elaine, who was in both classes. Another way to determine what was not understood was more private. All four students told about just ruminating on confusing passages or points made in class. Sometimes they were able to figure out what was being discussed, sometimes not. Sophie in particular mentioned abandoning the effort to make something out and just hoping she would not be asked about it on a test.

Apart from these limited instances, the questions on learning checks that Carmin encountered were so elementary that she considered them busywork. Before she even got to the learning check, she had already determined the desired concepts and connections just by reading or listening in class because, at least in part, she was manipulating automatically as she went along. Being forced to deduce what she had already deducted was a good part of the lack of challenge that motivated her disillusionment with her major.

Finally, sometimes, as in mnemonic tricks, the connections created can be meaningless. Carmin's use of mnemonics was limited to only one case, the definitions of *reality*.

Carmin: Oh, I didn't know if that was something you'd be interested in, but for the way to define reality, I listed them and then took the first letter out of each of the different ways and made a word of it, and that's how I memorized it. I didn't know if that would be important to you or not.

The use of these types of strategies was quite limited, even though Will's study-skills books and video recommended them. He had by this quarter abandoned all these tricks as ineffective.

DISPLAY

Display of information consists of the student's own expression of the content. This expression takes place in two contexts. One is the endgame, when it is done to receive points in what professors and researchers usually consider assessments. The other is when it is done for the student's own eyes, as in practice or notes.

Practice and Notes

Display as practice served as a check on comprehension. Greg, for example, was mistrustful of a mere sense or feeling of understanding:

Investig.: How much do you rely on a sense that, "Oh, I understand that," that "ah ha" sensation that sometimes people talk about?

Greg: Number one, if I have proved to myself that I have a handle on it, you know prior conversation and usually in a conversation or in written work where I have to write something and don't even look at notes or anything but come straight out with it and if it was all up there, that will give me a clue that I've got it.

Sophie, by contrast, never realized the unreliability of a feeling that she understood, and so she was unable to realize this need for displays of some kind before being tested. She continually encountered "cases where you know you explain it to me a certain way, and I thought I had understood the way he explained, and then it was wrong" on a test. Another reason for students to display information was as notes of some kind for later retrieval, that is, as a kind of supplement to memory. We have seen display, which was combined with extraction and sometimes manipulation, in the notes shown. They serve mainly to feed back into exposure, and this will be discussed in more detail in the section on lectures of the next chapter.

Endgame

The most prominent form of display could be found in its high-stakes incarnation as assessment. Any assignment, test, or paper that receives a grade can be understood as a form of information display, and the proposal here is that it is useful to view it this way in examining what students do. There were a number of forms (really genres) that assessment took in this study:

- Test questions, subdivided into multiple-choice items, essay questions, and short-answer questions.
- Written papers, short two-page responses, essays, and summaries of presentations.
- Oral presentations done in groups.
- Written exercises, answering book problem sets, and more advanced assignments designed to be done on computer.

The genre of assessment determined the processes used to create it, so the four students made it their business to know which forms they would be confronting as early in the process as they could. Professors, for their part, obliged students in this request by describing just how many questions on a test would be multiple choice versus short answer or essay, or the desired length of a reaction paper.

Some of the issues raised here have already been discussed in detail in the last chapter, in particular how the different types of test questions afforded different ways of displaying knowledge of concepts and the metainformational issues involved in short essays. There is of course a vast literature on extended writing. So I will close this chapter with an extensive discussion of genres that have received less attention: test questions, both multiple choice and essay varieties.

The multiple-choice format is ubiquitous in U.S. education, so it may require a certain amount of conscious distancing for some American educators to realize just how bizarre it is to display knowledge by selecting one choice from among four after a short prompt. In fact, this format is quite unusual outside the United States, and at least in Europe it has a sometimes sinister reputation. In my eight years living in Spain, I encountered it only on the driver's written exam, and it has a special name, "test" as in English. It is also no secret, of course, that its standardized incarnation has given birth to an entire industry designed to exploit its weaknesses, particularly in East Asia and among the U.S. upper-middle classes. Note how the notion of "beating the test" generally refers to multiple-choice rather than essay or short-answer exams, and of course there are issues of discrimination that have long plagued the testing industry. Interestingly, two of the five instructors we interviewed apologized for the use of multiple choice and kept it to a minimum. A third avoided it entirely. All these points provide reasons to believe that, as a genre, the multiple-choice test item is often thought of as the least valid form of measuring students' learning among faculty and students.

Many of linguistic problems associated with these tests have been analyzed by Hill and colleagues (Hill 1992, 1995, 2000a, 2000b; Hill and Larsen 2000). For one thing, they found that the choice is determined by the wording of the prompt and the distractors as well as the target. However, they have focused on standardized tests rather than on the instructor-created variety used in college classes, which are both less carefully crafted and more commonly encountered. Still, much of the following analysis owes a debt to this work.

The students in this study generally encountered multiple-choice items as a portion of a midterm or final exam, and the items varied greatly in quality. I discussed one factor determining item effectiveness in Chapter 6, which was related to the question of the functional view of concepts. In that chapter, I provided evidence that the most effective way to display knowledge of how a concept can be used was to provide an opportunity to apply the concept to a fictional situation. By contrast, attempts to use concepts to explain facts about the world—the most common type of concept-related multiple-choice item—were far less successful. The same could be said for items that involved descriptions of concepts.

Now I want to focus on an issue that I only touched on there: how multiple-choice items could often be deduced by internal coherence alone, quite apart from curricular content. The following two examples are from my usual source of illustrations of bad multiple-choice design, Carmin's Human Development midterms:

(1) Carol Gilligan's [*sic*] challenges the traditional theorists (Freud, Erikson). Which of the following criteria was a basis of her criticism?

(a) The inclusion of women as subjects was inappropriate.

(b) The order of the stages was accurate for everyone.

(c) Gender specific assumptions were used appropriately.

(d) The cultural context of the research was biased.

(2) Parental use of drugs influences the development of a fetus. The extent of the damage of drug use is influenced by several factors. Which of the following combinations best describes the variables which suggest the extent of risk to the fetus?

(a) Nature of the drug.

(b) Nature of the drug and timing of exposure.

(c) Nature of the drug, timing of exposure, and amount of exposure.

(d) Nature of the drug, timing of exposure, amount of exposure, and legal status of the drug (illegal/legal).

In item (1), choices *b* and *c* are not bases for criticisms at all. Choice *a* may be framed as a criticism, but it not a very convincing one. It is difficult to see why the inclusion of females should be criticized. Only *d* is a reasonable response. In item (2), only choice *c* provides likely factors for someone with basic knowledge of pregnancy and human biology. Alternatively, misleading wording could lead a student astray despite the fact that the student had considerable content area knowledge. The following example, again from Carmin's Human Development class, illustrates how lexical choice can become a problem:

(3) Preschool children's biosocial development is reflected in their motor skill development. Which of the following differentiates the preschooler's development in contrast to the infant and toddler development?

(a) Gross motor skills become more specialized in precision. Actions of previous stages acquire strength, coordination, and balance.

(b) Fine motor skill focus on eye and brain coordination which requires strength, dexterity, and strategic planning.

(c) Master play becomes basic motivation to a child's activity.

(d) All of the above.

In principle, this item seems to require extensive knowledge of a number of concepts, distributed between item and choice. However, despite the fact that Carmin was in control of these concepts, she chose *c* in place of the target *d*. She described her reasoning as follows:

Carmin: The first time I read through it, I checked them all because I
   thought they all apply to preschoolers, and then I read through, and I
   saw that it was supposed to *differentiate* preschool from the others,
   and then I chose *c* because I didn't think *a* and *b* differentiated at all.

While no other exam came close to these as illustrations of what
could go wrong when a multiple-choice exam writer is careless, the
issues involved were not limited to that class. Recall that a related
problem was discussed in example (2) on page 72, where Greg picked
a distractor because the stem combined with the target formed an
ungrammatical sentence. The remaining two students were also
sometimes led to pick a distractor by the wording of multiple-choice
items in other ways. Will, who once scored at a C+ level on the
multiple-choice section of a Political Science midterm but got a full
forty points out of forty on the essay portion, worried about being
led astray by tempting choices. He described how he would "read
the question and not really look at the answers because a lot of
times I think that the answers can lead you away from the correct
one."

To return to a thread begun in Chapter 6, the basic problem with
the multiple-choice design is that it forces all information into a
propositional and therefore factual format. Some of the problems
created are so obvious, as in the examples from Carmin's Human
Development exam, that they require little analysis to understand.
In the other exams, by contrast, they were usually more subtle,
and it is not as easy to see precisely why they pose problems for
some students. All four students were at one point or another tripped
up by wording, but Sophie had particular problems in this area.
She described how she preferred items with short choices because
those with long ones confused her. There were cases when the words
of a choice became such a jumble for her that she was no longer
reading what the item said but taking a stab in the dark as to the
meaning based on different words.

On that point, while it is often assumed by students as well as
critics of traditional assessment that multiple-choice test taking is
a skill, it is not easy to see what such a skill would consist of. To do
so requires a semantic analysis of the items that gets below the
surface. Such an analysis would reveal how an item can be successfully parsed and how a test taker can go wrong. I would like to
propose here that it is possible, using some situation-theoretic tools
described in Chapter 6, to explore some of these confusions in detail.
In that chapter, I explained the way that it is possible to write facts
formulaically in situation-theoretic terms. Recall that in situation-
theoretic terms, facts consist of one type of what in the theory are

known as *infons*, or basic units of information. Recall that an infon
has an internal structure consisting of the assertion of a *relation-*
ship among various *arguments*, or entities or concepts, and that
this structure is captured in the following formulaic terms:

$$\sigma = <<R, a_1, \ldots a_n>>$$

The σ represents the infon, which breaks down into R, which
represents the relation, and the arguments represented by a; the
subscripts *1* through n serve to distinguish one argument from the
other. The arguments themselves can consist of things, people, locations, times, polarity (i.e., *yes* or *no*), or other infons. This last
possibility allows us to embed one infon inside another, much as
we can put a clause inside another clause in grammar. The advantage of this formulaic notation is that it constitutes a semantic representation that permits the description of the complexity of the
information. Take as an example the following item from Sophie's
Political Science midterm:

(4) A factor accounting for the higher voter turnout in Australia and Great
Britain compared to the United States is . . .

(a) the lack of meaningful party choice in Australia and Britain.

(b) more demanding residency requirements in Australia and Britain.

(c) less demanding registration procedures in Australia and Britain.

(d) a more educated electorate in Australia and Britain.

The target was *c* but Sophie chose *b*, although quite apart from
course content this choice is incoherent.[3] After all, how could strin-
gency of residence requirements possibly increase voter turnout?
It is interesting to explore what Sophie had to say retrospectively
about it, particularly since she had gone to her TA to discuss why
she had gotten it wrong. In other words, even after receiving the
test back and going over it, she was unable to decipher what was
being asked in this item and had to ask the TA.

Sophie: I had a real problem with that because in Australia, it's required
that you vote. It's not you know a freedom, like in the United States. And
so the way the answers are worded, *b* and *c*, my choice was between
the two and I couldn't tell which one, so I just kind of guessed *b*. . . .
[Nevertheless] "more demanding residency requirements in Australia and Britain" was wrong because they don't have lots of requirements as far as residency goes, that you don't need to live there for so
long, and I didn't look at the answer being that way. I was looking at
the words "demanding residency requirements" and "demanding reg-

istration procedures," which to me meant the same thing, but residency requirements [the TA] was pointing out to me was wrong, and was different from registration procedures. There's no residency requirement in Australia and Britain, and in the United States, registration procedures are a pain in the butt. I mean you gotta go to the court house and poll to sign up and all that good stuff, and you don't have to do that there.

My argument is that Sophie saw her task on this item as a kind of matching. She wanted to match her remembered fact, "Voting is required in Australia," with a proposition that she would construct from the item stem and the choices she considered:

A factor accounting for the higher voter turnout in Australia and Great Britain compared to the United States is more demanding residency requirements in Australia and Britain.

or

A factor accounting for the higher voter turnout in Australia and Great Britain compared to the United States is less demanding registration procedures in Australia and Britain.

As propositions, these "stem + choice" combinations can be analyzed as infons, and doing so allows us to break down the reasoning needed to arrive at the target choice. In this case, it shows just how complex and elaborate this reasoning is, and it offers a plausible explanation as to why Sophie, and students like her, make these kinds of errors.

I will illustrate this complexity by breaking down the distractor, *b* which Sophie chose, step by step. When an embedded infon is an argument, I will do so by writing σ, in one of the argument positions. I distinguish the infons from one another with numeric subindexes. I also apologize in advance to readers allergic to formulas for the use of this notation, but I know of no other way to make the relations clear and comparable.

In the first step, for example, the relation *accounts for* holds between two infons:

$$<<\text{Accounts for}, \sigma_1, \sigma_2, 1>>$$

The next step analyzes the first of these infons into its component parts. In this case, the relation *more than* holds between two other infons (i.e., there is more of one than the other):

$$\sigma_1 = <<\text{More than}, \sigma_3, \sigma_4, 1>>$$

For the third step, we analyze σ_3 and σ_4, determining that there are *demanding registration requirements* in Australia and Britain on the one hand, and in the United States on the other:

σ_3 = <<demanding, registration requirements, Australia and Britain>>

σ_4 = <<demanding, registration requirements, United States>>

With the first argument of the matrix proposition fully analyzed, we return to σ_2, which breaks down into an infon parallel to the σ_1:

$$\sigma_2 = \text{<<more than, } \sigma_6, \sigma_7 \text{>>}$$

The breakdown is completed with an analysis of σ_6 and σ_7:

σ_6 = <<voting, people, Australia and Britain>>

σ_7 = <<voting, people, United States>>

As if this informational structure weren't complex enough, Sophie then proposes to connect it with the memorized proposition *Voting is compulsory in Australia,* despite the imperfect fit created by the absence of Britain. Finally, she needs to perform this kind of analysis without any opportunity to use contextual redundancy to repair small imprecisions. Given this tangle of arguments, Sophie seems to simply have given up trying to sort out exactly what information was on offer. Instead, she just focused on one part of the mess, the fact that *more demanding* is semantically similar to *requirements.* The arguments, *registration procedures* and *residency requirements*, were entirely forgotten, and she was thus unable to separate the two choices. In fact, the whole matching operation was unnecessary. Since, as I said earlier, the choice is incoherent because more demanding residency requirements cannot account for higher voter turnout.

In support of this view, five out of the six multiple-choice items Sophie missed on this test were long and semantically elaborate such as this one. By contrast, she only missed one with choices of a nonembedded phrase or one-word length. Finally, she was quite aware of her difficulties, and claimed that when faced with long choices, she either panicked or resorted to series of linguistic-based strategies only distantly related to meaning as described in the last chapter.

Sophie's poor multiple-choice test taking consisted of a number of missteps. She believed that she needed to match her remembered fact to an item, and she did not realize the advantage of looking first for item incoherence as a way of eliminating potential distractors. Besides eliminating some choices, it is a lot easier to break down the meaning of this kind of complex item when a test taker is not trying to match it with a remembered fact and simultaneously parse its complex informational structure. Greg and Carmin largely performed this type of thinking about tangled decontextualized propositions competently and quickly, but Will, along with Sophie, frequently failed to do so.

Situation theory provides a way to understand some of the difficulties the multiple-choice format presents to some students. Conversely, this kind of close analysis also explains the ability of more test-wise students to find target responses to items they have little knowledge about solely on the basis of coherence. Surely no one wishes to produce tests that are unfair or test informational parsing instead of, say, Physics, and this kind of analysis could provide test makers with factors to consider in producing these kinds of items that can avoid creating unnecessary difficulties in parsing. Similarly, semantic analysis of items can help uncover strategies that test takers should consider when they do encounter them.

Compared to multiple-choice items, short essays presented fewer problems for the students in this study. For one thing, as I mentioned in the sections on concepts and connections in Chapter 6, it is far easier to explicate these forms of information when the displays are not crammed into a single proposition. This greater leeway was employed most effectively by Greg, who did not limit himself to language but used diagrams on at least two questions, one in Statistics and the other in Methods. Still, these items do have very strict genre rules. Most prominent of these that appeared on the participants' exams was the importance for the test taker to identify the concepts or connections being elicited and provide the grader with the expected information about them. This information had to be provided even when it was peripheral to actually answering the question. Greg, who had problems being explicit enough on his statistics exercises (see p. 97), had few doubts about being exhaustive on essay questions. Note his answer to the following item from a Statistics test (the information on the top was used for several items):

Annual income of individuals in Brazil	Annual income of individuals in Thailand
x = 2600	x = 850
s = $790	s = $410
median = 2000	median = 800

In a couple of sentences, briefly explain why the mean annual income in Brazil is higher than the median annual income in Brazil. Be specific.

Greg's Answer: If the income in Brazil were distributed normally the median annual income would be the same as the average annual income. The median at $2000 means that 1/2 of the Brazilians earn less than $2000 and 1/2 earn more than $2,000. The average of $2,600, which is above the median, means that there is a skewed distribution; that is, there are more extreme income values on the high end of the income spectrum than on the low end.

A couple of landowners with incomes of $100,000/yr will inflate the average.

Only one connection, a difference between mean and median, is explicitly requested, and Greg provides that connection in his response, but then this connection is treated as a concept through illustration with an example. Following that, *mean* and *median*— two presumed target concepts underlined in the prompt and used in the connection—are also defined in terms of the data. In addition, other related concepts that are not even mentioned (i.e., normal distribution, skewed distribution) are also used, though not defined. The result got full credit.

Carmin also got full credit for her answer to a question on the Human Development midterm requiring her to apply five concepts to a picture of a two-year old leading a blind grandmother in a poor African village. The caption to the picture said that the toddler's parents were also blind. In fact, Carmin supplied seven concepts, and a few of them seemed to be a bit of a stretch if the question was taken at face value. These additions included "child abuse," which she declared to "not be a problem" because "the parents would have a need for the child and would highly value" her. Also, Carmin included "Freud's anal stage" because the girl had "high demand for maturity" due to her leading her blind family members around. This last sentence got the comment "important point" from the grader. Nevertheless, it is somehow hard to imagine an actual social worker, even the most unreconstructed Freudian, going to such a village and considering the anal stage as a major issue in a needs analysis. It seems far more likely that the grader was responding to the creative way in which Carmin inserted this central concept into the answer. Finally, Carmin assigned the little girl "malnutrition" because of the "bloating of [the girl's] stomach," although the picture, a black and white photocopy of a photo, was of too poor quality for one to be sure of that. In any case, regardless of whether these applications were somewhat strained, they contained clear, consistent definitions of the concepts applied.

Poor essays, by contrast, tended to be unclear in their elucidations of concepts. An extreme example was Will's sketchy discussion of statistical significance shown on page 96. Of course, not all essay questions involve concepts. In Chapter 6, I described Greg's History final, which elicited largely facts that were minimally connected together. In fact, use of concepts was dangerous on this essay because if the instructor did not approve of the way they were used it was possible to lose points.

The lesson to be learned from these cases is that the point is not to take the essay question at face value. Instead, it is to use the response as a vehicle for delivering whatever information the test taker determines that the grader will reward. The test taker's first task upon reading the question is to determine what that information is. In most cases encountered by the case-study students, it involved descriptions and applications of concepts, although it could in principle be any type of information at all, as in the facts on Greg's History exams.

I will close with a final feature of the game-like nature of attempts to score points—the equivalent of a technical foul. Besides cheating, which I did not encounter, students can lose points for not following certain rules. For example, Greg received a warning on one of his Statistics exercises advising him that if he handed one in at the end rather than at the beginning of the period again, he would lose 10 percent. The stricter or looser enforcement of such rules obviously enters into a student's calculations on any assignment not done in class.

NOTES

1. In fairness, Wittgenstein's discussion here is really of images. However, his discussion of more conceptual "pictures" appears to be related. See especially pages 422–427.

2. I have heard the same process being used to create conference abstracts. One linguist colleague told me admiringly that his coauthor was a master at anticipating and pandering to reviewers' prejudices. Both their abstracts were indeed accepted to a highly selective conference, which is not to say that they lacked quality.

3. Note that choice *a* is also incoherent as a possible answer.

Chapter 8

Playing the Game

In the past two chapters, I explored operations and information types as components of a game consisting of channeling course content from a source to a goal. These two sets of categories provide better access to what is happening as students take courses than does a descriptive analysis alone or one using less precise categories such as study strategies or text types. Nevertheless, the focus in each case was on the role of the operation or type of information, which can give the mistaken impression that types of information and operations act in isolation. Nothing could be further from the truth. In this chapter, therefore, I show how information types and operations interacted by widening the angle of the lens so to speak, and starting with a less highly theorized depiction of the study activities. In so doing, I reveal aspects of the participants' academic life that were missed in the close-in examinations of formal categories. I do this by looking at the game in three main stages, procuring information, channeling it, and displaying it for a grade in what I called in the last chapter "the endgame."

PROCURING INFORMATION

Students can first get information in one or two main formats: written or oral. The predominantly oral sources included, in order of frequency, lectures, discussions in recitation, conversations with classmates or professors, videos, and student presentations. Written ones consisted of, also in order of frequency, textbooks, instructor-produced copies of various kinds, trade books (e.g., novels, nonfiction, plays), and finally scholarly articles.[1]

Classes and Readings

The oral/written division turned out to be significant in several ways. First, participants displayed a striking preference for lectures over reading. In part, this predilection might have been a response to the fact that a lecture provides more help in extraction than a textbook does. After all, if information was mentioned by a professor, it was more likely to be requested on an exam than if it just appeared in an assignment. The professor preselects some content. However, the participants also appeared to exhibit a greater comfort with an oral over a written channel quite apart from this advantage. This preference was apparent to Professor Haus, who was the most insightful and interested faculty member with regards to his students' learning and studying. In the first chapter, I quoted him as saying, "Students don't read; they can't read; they don't want to read; and they don't get as much out of it" as they do lectures. Now is a good time to evaluate his lamentation in more detail.

First, while it is not literally true that the participants 'didn't read' their assignments, not a single one even came close to doing all the required readings in their courses. In the final interview, Carmin actually admitted that early in the quarter the only reason she had read at times was "because I knew I was going to have to come and talk to somebody about how much reading I did." This is admittedly a blatant, though unintentional, effect of the research on the behavior being studied. However, it can more positively also be seen as evidence that Carmin believed that she would not otherwise be complying with some external norm (i.e., doing her assignments) that she did not really think she needed to follow just to succeed.

There is also some evidence to support Professor Haus's second complaint that "they can't read" if his words are again not taken literally but as referring to some lower-than-expected ability. Greg, who by all rights should have been the most able reader based on his academic success, was surprisingly limited in his repertoire of reading approaches. During the quarter, he reported reading no more than ten pages per hour. He believed that his slow rate was owed to the fact that he read too deeply, "thinking about every paragraph." Using the taxonomy of operations, he overused manipulation as he read. This was an advantage in a way, as he described his way of creating a mental movie to go with Ivan Denisovich that would help him remember what happened. However, in the case of expository writing he would end up exploring all the conceptual angles suggested by a text. He found this process frustrating and asked, "Should I just be skimming it? Should I just read those last sentences of each paragraph?" He did not seem to know, even after four years and a 3.85 GPA. Nor was he aware that he might read through without thinking of every connection or concept implied in a reading, or even understanding every fact. Only Carmin had a consistent system for reading that would be recognizable from a study-skills perspective, and even that was a rudimentary one; she read and highlighted. Again using the taxonomy, she consistently linked extraction with exposure. She manipulated when necessary to understand and thought automatically about implications.

In the third clause, Professor Haus claimed that his undergraduates "don't want to read." It was certainly true that given an alternative (i.e., whenever the information was available in a spoken format) that form would take precedence for them. Will put it in terms of consumer's rights: "I'd rather use the book as a back up rather than as a tool for learning. That's why I feel I pay; I pay a professor to teach me." Sophie assumed the same posture of letting lectures lead and reported that when the readings did not seem to relate to lecture content, she stopped looking at the book. "It really upset me," she reported, when she did not see the connection between lecture and book in Political Science. "I'm like quitting. It didn't make sense to me why I have to read things like that, so I didn't read it."

Insofar as Dr. Haus's last claim, that they "don't get as much out of it" as they do out of lectures, there were several ways in which this appeared to be the case. First, Greg certainly did understand and profit from his readings. However, he reported, "I can't seem to get through" some assigned readings; this was because of his slow reading rate. Will, on the other extreme of academic success, often had trouble just making sense of readings, and his efforts to deal with this problem seemed to vary by subject area. In Biology, instead of finding out the connections or concepts he was missing, he tended to classify much of his reading as "just a bunch of gibberish; it's just basically filler, the BS." Will's first tendency was to look for facts, and he wanted the key facts laid out for him, which the text and professor would not or could not do. His depiction of this seemingly unorganized mass of content as "filler" and "BS" gave him the rationalization he needed to ignore large portions of the text. On the other hand, in psychology he realized he was lacking in concepts and made an effort—only really successful toward the end of the quarter—to ferret out the missing elements.

Their bias toward oral language could also be noted in that they would often skip readings when they determined that those were redundant relative to lectures rather than, say, stop attending lectures and only read, even in large lecture classes that afforded considerable anonymity. In other words, if the material was too distant, it might be left unread, but if it was too similar, then it also would not be read. For example, in the middle of the quarter the lecturer in the Chemistry class, which was being team-taught, changed, and Sophie announced that she was no longer reading in that class either. "It's just too monotonous to read the book anymore, you know; I just follow his notes and lecture, and he's really good. He's a better lecturer I think than the other one was." Will read everything only in Psychology because the exams could be on material that was not covered in lecture. In Changing Family and Methods, Greg also read sporadically and again based on what specific information he thought he might need that he did not get from lecture. The only exceptions to this tendency to skip readings over classes involved emotional responses by Greg to his two other classes. In History, Greg read but did not attend lectures for several weeks. In Statistics, he first read the book in class, and then after he was spotted doing that he cut class only to read the material being covered there in the classroom next door. This embarrassing incident is discussed in more detail in the following paragraphs.

It should be no surprise that how much students got out of the readings was closely related to their interest and therefore the time and energy they put into them. What was less expected was that the effects of motivation were a lot less pronounced with lectures for three of the four students. Apart from Greg, the participants could dislike a lecturer, but they would still diligently go to class and take notes and then go to recitation and listen or participate. Another symptom of their better concentration when listening than when reading can be found in the fact that all four students reported coming to the ends of pages at times and realizing that they had not been paying any attention to the content. They would then have to go back and reread. By contrast, no one reported drifting away during lectures, which I found personally surprising since I recall a quite rich classroom fantasy life. So in the end, Carmin only missed one Human Development class and Methods class and no Theatre or Policy classes or any recitations. Even Sophie, hardly the model student, rarely skipped classes, and Will did so only for medical reasons.

The participants were quite aware of their predilection for listening over reading. Even Greg, the exception with regard to assiduous class attendance, claimed that the oral encoding was crucial:

"There is a big aspect to learning from hearing something. It does stick for me sometimes a little better if someone is talking. . . . I learn from verbal stimulus." In this he was echoed by Will, who claimed that auditory memory was essential. Will told about how he would hear something a professor had said over in his mind when looking at his notes, which brought back the entire physical experience of the classroom.

Of course, as I am sure many readers are aware, there is no shortage of students who regularly miss classes, and I make no claims for typicality on the basis of these four, or better, the three excluding Greg. However, I would suggest as a hypothesis that when U.S. students are seriously engaged in the achievement game, they may be far less likely to miss a class than they are to skip a reading. In other words, "cutting" a class, far more than "blowing off" a reading, is likely a sign of withdrawal from the academic-achievement game. This interpretation is supported by the fact that the students in this study differentiated themselves from less serious colleagues in part because they attended class regularly. Greg's disengagement from History and Statistics should be seen in light of this ideological role of attendance in the case-study students' definition of what counts as taking courses seriously. More than just a lack of interest in the material or calculation of informational profit from attendance, his refusal to go to class constituted a kind of protest statement that skipping readings just would not have made.

The affect-driven nature of this behavior can be seen in the embarrassing incident I referred to earlier. During the third week, at the height of Greg's rebellion against the grading system in general and against his Statistics class in particular, he began a somewhat bizarre practice. He went to class, put earplugs in his ears, and proceeded to follow along with the class topic in the previous edition of the textbook, which he had taken out of the library. (Recall that he had sold his textbook.) The idea seems to have been to be sure that he spent the due time on Statistics without actually acceding entirely to the system that had forced him into a class he did not believe he needed.[2] During the fourth week he duly went to the class and put his earplugs in and began to read. In the midst of lecture, Professor Tomko came around to adjust a light switch and found him there with his earplugs in looking intently at the book. Suddenly becoming aware of her presence, he looked up in horror and received a funny look in return, which left him even more flustered. The next class, he decided to read in the room next to class, which was empty, and in that way he would force himself to keep up without giving in to the system. This was followed a week later by another blow: an actually failing midterm grade. A semicontrite Greg decided that he needed to reassess his defiant posture. "Clearly, something was not learned," he admitted. These events became a kind of a turning point in the resistance to academic authority. Once the exam was returned, he began to attend regularly and without earplugs.

However, the reading panorama was not uniformly bleak. Occasionally, Greg reported wanting to read more in depth out of pure interest, particularly for the Changing Family class, but he rarely if ever did so because he always felt pressed for time. Carmin enjoyed the plays she read for Theatre. Will also found interest in reading, particularly for Psychology, where the class read from a book of case studies by, as he put it, "actual psychologists." Even Sophie reported having liked some readings in the past when the classes actually interested her. Additionally, they all expressed appreciation for clear expositions in textbooks.

In any case, whatever their preferences, these students at times had no choice but to do some reading to get a handle on the information, and they knew and accepted that fact. They also knew that they could pay dearly when they underestimated the amount of reading they needed to do, which did not prevent them from making that error on occasion. Carmin miscalculated in Theatre, Greg did in Statistics, and Sophie did in Political Science, although Greg and Carmin at least accepted the resulting low grades as just desserts. Sophie's case is more complex and will be dealt with in the next section.

It does not have to be this way. In contrast to these four students, the Catalan undergraduates studied by Mireia Trenchs in Newman, Trenchs, and Pujol (under review) showed a much richer repertoire of reading strategies and approaches. They also valued written text above oral discourse, preferring their readings over lectures and even finding additional unassigned readings occasionally. They had been systematically trained since school in how to read for information and interpretation, and they were part of a culture in which certain written texts held a high iconic value.

How and When to Read

Whatever a student's feelings, reading allows them a great deal more flexibility with regard to manipulation and extraction than a lecture does. Evidently, the text and so the information it contains do not just vanish as the words in a lecture do. With flexibility comes choice, and whenever the students did decide to read, they were faced with two decisions. The first was how deep to go—how much to manipulate and extract. Intensity can vary from simple skimming, on the one end, to reading that emphasized manipulation to ferret out initially all manner of hidden or opaque meanings, on the other. Somewhere in between they could combine exposure with a form of extraction, such as highlighting. Another possibility was to combine it with extraction and display in writing glosses and notes, although this was rare. Only Greg did so, and his notes often had little to do with what he imagined would be on an exam but had more to do with his own intellectual curiosity and interests. Thus, he had more such combinations in the Changing Family class than in any other course.

As we have seen, Greg only read intensively, meaning that he used a lot of manipulation, in particular making connections between the information in the text and previous knowledge or other parts of the text. Generalizing from the particulars of his own experience, he believed that "the required reading wouldn't get done unless someone dedicated every single waking hour to studying, which is what I used to do." To save time, therefore, he simply did not read large portions of required chapters and instead skillfully relied on cues in classes or instructions for exams to determine what he would read. In the case of Changing Family, he read little of what appeared on the exam, until the very day the take-home midterm was handed out. He began with extraction before actually reading. This coping tactic was moderately successful considering how last-minute it was, since he received a respectable but hardly stellar B+ in the course.

The only exceptions were History and Statistics, where he read the textbooks instead of going to class for a few weeks. The history book was a standard survey that presented no conceptual challenges; persons, events, and ideas were simply presented in narrative format. This tactic worked fine. In Statistics, however, it did not. Statistics turned out to be a lot more challenging than History, despite Greg's belief that the class was mostly duplicating what he had learned earlier. Greg had little systemacity in terms of when he read, which appears to derive from a perceived lack of need. Note the cockiness evident in the following exchange during the first week of the quarter:

Investig.: Do you do the reading before each class, for example before the lecture or after, or how do you do it?

Greg: That sounds like a good plan; I'd like to do that. In practice I haven't read anything for this quarter yet. I will be shortly. Do you care about reasons?

Investig.: Yeah, tell me the reasons.

Greg: Reasons, yeah ok. I guess I've been busy enough meeting people in
   Tecumseh, getting in touch with old friends, spending time with my
   roommate, and getting my apartment in order. So I haven't read yet,
   and I don't feel bothered about it, and I will start reading soon. . . . I'm
   gonna be interested in learning something, and I'm gonna have to
   start doing something.

In fact, many times he, like Carmin, read only just before the exam
or even after he had been given a take home exam as in his Changing Family seminar. Of course pride came, as it should, before the
fall, even if the only serious difficulties took place in Statistics.

Sophie skimmed, read in front of the television, and almost
stopped reading entirely half way through the quarter. Not surprisingly, this lack of attention nearly led to an academic train
wreck, only buffered by grade inflation. In fact, three essays and
five multiple-choice items on the Political Science midterm required
use examples from the book, which Sophie did not have at hand, so
she ended up supplying her own.[3] Her response to the resulting
lost points was to complain to the TA about her examples on the
essay questions not counting. Yet even after that fruitless appeal,
she still did not realize (or did not admit) that she had lost points
because her examples were from the lecture or experience instead
of the book. Instead, she claimed, albeit sheepishly, that the grading was just unfair and the TA's criteria inscrutable.

In terms of time, Sophie's decision on when to read depended on
the class. In the Political Science course, she said, "Reading ahead
before he talks about it in class really helps. But I have to listen in
chemistry first and then read the book." The reason was that she
was really unable to get much of a handle on the Chemistry text
without first having heard it. Once they changed professors mid-
way through the quarter, Sophie abandoned Chemistry reading
entirely, of course, except for right before the exam.

Carmin was the only student who was systematic in her initial
reading—when she decided to do it—although the system itself
changed. Going into the quarter she said, "A lot of times, I'll read
what's supposed to be read just before I go to class." Soon, however,
she found that the content of the classes did not require such assiduousness. Then she let the class lead, and when she believed
something was not important, she skimmed or did not read at all.
When even that much proved more reading than was needed and
she had gotten over the sense that she needed to read for the interviews—about halfway through the quarter—she limited reading to
a review procedure just before a test.

Will began the quarter enunciating the same strategy as Carmin;
he would read before class and so be prepared for the lecture. In

fact, in the tradition of best-laid plans, he soon seemed to have forgotten entirely about this strategy and also tended to use the lecture to guide the reading. If material was covered in lecture, it needed to be read. As a result, he felt a bad lecture that left the various points unclear could "really destroy my reading process." He also expressed a desire several times to always read intensively. However, his notion of intense was not the same as Greg's; manipulation was largely absent from Will's reading because of his photographic definition of remembering. He wanted to concentrate hard on each item of information and thereby have it lodge in his memory.

And so, despite the various students' stumbles owing to their lack of reading, it seems fair to say that apart from a few classes, Midwestern State can be a quite forgiving place with regard to students' reading sins.

In Class

Lectures and recitations, the two forms that classes took, have predominantly though not exclusively oral formats. Written language appears usually on a chalkboard or an overhead. In the International Relations class, the overheads systematically displayed during the lectures were repeated in the course packet, and all together they depicted an orderly schema of the entire curriculum. In class, these overheads functioned something like a jazz score off which Professor Haus would do some informational riffs but always return to. Other classes varied between some overheads, some not-very-systematic blackboard writing, occasional handouts, and pure talking. The lack of written accompaniment could lead to what I would call either the "Chow Chesque" or "Eyende" effect after Sophie's invented spelling of the hapless Romanian and Chilean presidents' names; this will be discussed later in this section. Still the students had no particular preferences as to one or another of these formats—apart from Will's appreciation of Professor Haus's overhead projector work and packet—and in any case the spoken channel predominated. There was more talk than chalk (or plastic film).

Lectures differed from recitations in (1) the size of the class, which could be much larger in a lecture than a recitation; (2) the amount of interaction—with there being far more in recitation than in lectures, particularly in courses containing both; and (3) hierarchy. Lectures were usually taught by doctoral faculty and recitations by graduate TAs. Consequently, lectures rather than recitations were primary sources of information. About half the classes had recitations, including Greg's Statistics and Methods, Will's Biology, and Sophie's Political Science and Chemistry.

Students appreciated lectures that were clear rather than exciting or interactive. It is worth noting on this point that instructors largely assumed a transmission pedagogy; there was little active learning taking place. The class with the most active learning was Carmin's Human Development course, in which students were sometimes placed into groups to solve problems and prepare an oral presentation. Carmin did not mind this relatively novel approach, but neither was she particularly impressed by it. Perhaps if she had had more need to manipulate the course content, she would have appreciated the opportunity that group work provides for doing so in class. Similarly, the other students did not complain about lack of active engagement, apart from Greg in his History course. However, this was a special case because there were political disputes involved, unrelated to the achievement game. Greg became infuriated that the instructor assumed a standard U.S. capitalist perspective misleadingly disguised, he asserted, as a recounting of objective facts. He wanted to add an alternative, more left-wing viewpoint, which the professor would not allow. At one lecture he reported having "listened for the first ten minutes and said [to himself], 'I feel like reading the book instead.'" Yet he also pointed out the disadvantages of the student-centered classrooms he had experienced in his year abroad in Germany. He said that since students did not know as much as professors and were less capable of expressing the knowledge they did have, he did not learn as much in the student-led classes.

The other three students mentioned several qualities they did not like in lectures. Will complained about getting lost when he would spend time trying to figure out the meaning of something his Biology professor said and then having trouble recovering the thread. Carmin thought her Policy professor just did not cover enough information. He wasted time and went off on tangents that had little to do with the subject matter, such as the notorious definitions of "reality." Sophie did not like what she felt were the misleading claims of relevance in her Political Science class, although she ended up accepting them somewhat in the end.

The predominantly oral format constrained what happened in lectures and recitation in terms of operations. Oral language is evanescent, unless the student tapes it as Will did, which means that students must take notes to preserve the information that lecturers convey, or at least (as I used to do) get the notes from someone in the class. Because it is impossible for any student to get down everything the professor says, it becomes necessary to extract much earlier than with a reading. Classes thus combined minimally extraction and display with exposure.

At the same time, this ongoing flow of information inhibited the ability of students to manipulate it as they encountered it. This could be bad, as when Will lost the thread of the Biology lectures as he tried to figure out what the professor was saying, but it could also work well to keep Greg's obsessive manipulations from getting out of hand. Will's insecurity in this area may be added to his desire to put off extraction as a motive to tape and transcribe lectures whole in the Psychology Writing and Biology classes. The result of his trying to remember everything was that he lost control of what information would actually stay with him. The only class in which Will felt he did not need to record was Political Science because of the guidance from Professor Haus's transparencies. In effect, he was happy to leave manipulation and extraction to the professor. He was not against extraction or manipulation on principle, it seems, so much as mistrustful of his own ability to perform them effectively. In the previous chapter, I showed how his own notes were practically verbatim copies of the professor's slides.

Greg's class notes, by contrast, combined extraction and display with manipulation. They almost always focused on interweaving connections and concepts. His notes from History thus matched those from Changing Family, shown in Chapter 7, although it was, he claimed, a fact-driven class (Figure 8.1). Again we find his characteristic pattern of creating a hierarchy of ideas, various graphic signals, including lines, arrows, and line length, that help carry the informational load and reflect his efforts to construct rather than merely record knowledge as he listened. Greg confirmed that he used this approach in a number of his classes. This is how he described his thinking in his Methods class:

Greg: In Methods . . . I paid attention in class and had often purposefully tried to construct that overarching perspective. "Where do all of these things fit in that he's talking about?" I would ask myself.

Thus he read and attended to lectures in this same way, but he could not rely on himself to keep the information moving when reading. He functioned better when there was someone else controlling the pace.

Sophie's notes were different again (Figure 8.2). She did not believe that she needed to "get it all" as Will did, but she had no clear criteria for deciding what to leave out, what to put down, and what to do with what she decided to keep. She also knew that she needed to manipulate by at least marking a hierarchical order, but that was also not easy for her. Her notes, therefore, tended to be sketchy and incomplete, looking as if she wrote catch-as-catch-can as the lecturer spoke.

Figure 8.1
Greg's History Notes

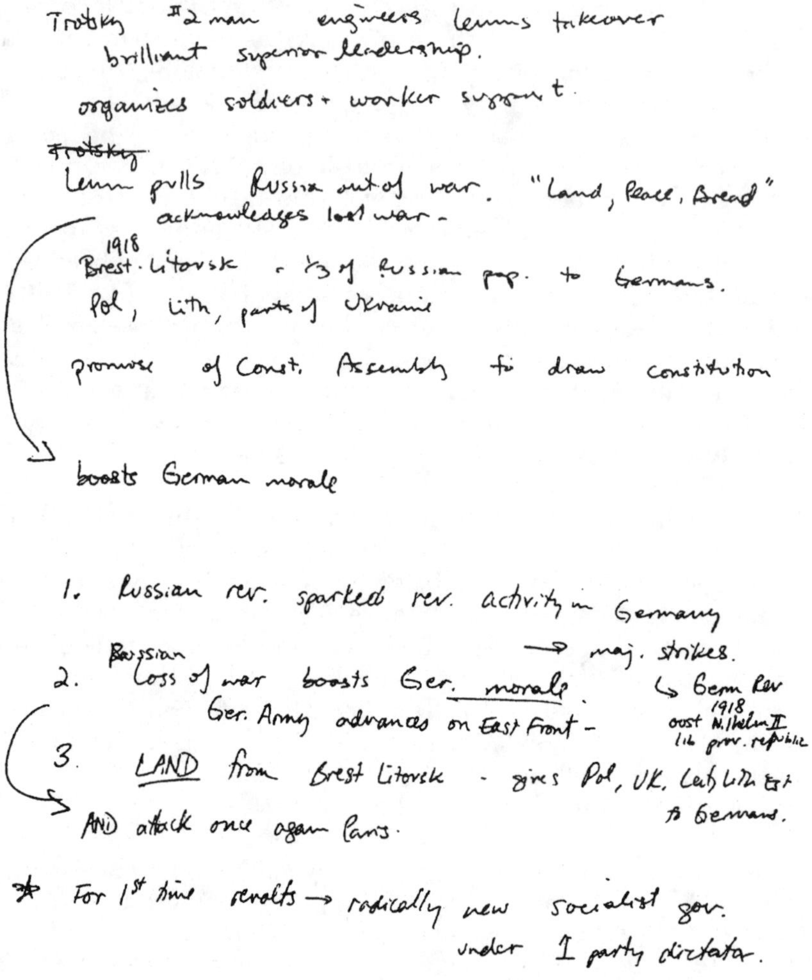

Trotsky   #2 man   engineers lenins takeover
brilliant superior leadership.

organizes soldiers + worker support.

~~Trotsky~~
Lenin pulls Russia out of war. "Land, Peace, Bread"
   acknowledges lost war -
   1918
Brest-Litovsk - 1/3 of Russian pop. to Germans.
Pol, Lith, parts of Ukraine

promise of Const. Assembly to draw constitution

boosts German morale

1. Russian rev. sparked rev. activity in Germany
                                    → maj. strikes.
2. Russian
   loss of war boosts Ger. morale.   ↳ Germ Rev
      Ger. Army advances on East Front -   1918
                                    oust Wilhelm II
                                    lib prov. republic
3. LAND from Brest Litovsk - gives Pol, UK, Lat, Lith Est
                                    to Germans.
   AND attack once again Paris.

* For 1st time revolts → radically new socialist gov.
                        under 1 party dictator.

In the extract from her Political Science notes, again covering historical material, the facts caught appear to be fairly random and incomplete. There was an effort to place those facts under conceptual headings in a concept-example format, but the examples look hasty and superficial. The concept of communism is exemplified by the countries of China, Cambodia, and Romania, and Romania is shown to be associated with Ceausescu, who, misspelling notwithstanding, is given the briefest of biographies.[4] The entire schema is so undeveloped that all that could be recovered is a few facts: "Cambodia is communist." "Ceaucescu grew up watching rich people." There are some rudimentary efforts at manipulation, but

Figure 8.2
Sophie's Political Science Notes

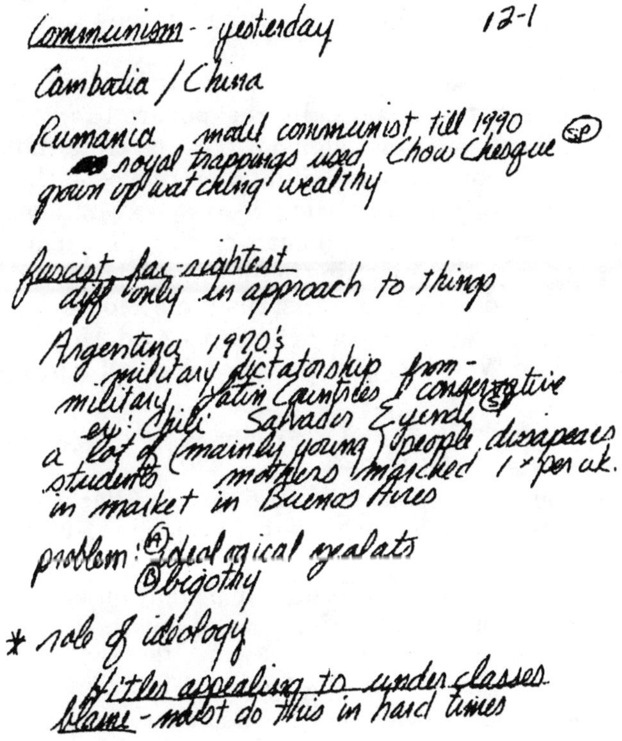

Communism - - yesterday 12-1
Cambodia / China
Rumania model communist till 1990
royal trappings used Chow Chesque
grown up watching wealthy

fascist far-rightest
diff only in approach to things

Argentina 1970's
military dictatorship from -
military Latin Countries conservative
ex: Chili Salvador Eyende
a lot of (mainly young) people disappeared
students mothers marched 1× per wk.
in market in Buenos Aires

problem: ideological zealots
bigotry

* role of ideology
Hitler appealing to under classes
blame - most do this in hard times

her attempt to create connections between concepts runs into difficulty. Communism differs from fascism only in its "approach to things." There are also problems of accuracy and coherence; it is not clear what "Hitler appealing to under classes blame" means or how it could exemplify the "role of ideology." When one considers that Sophie abandoned the class textbook and her review largely consisted of rereading these kinds of notes, often in front of the television, her C begins to look like an accomplishment, either that or a gift.

IN THE CHANNEL

Studying

Once the oral and/or written sources of the information have been encountered, the next step a student faces is how to be sure that the right information is under control and on its path to the assessment. This task can be tackled in a variety of ways, all of which tend to be classified under what the students called "studying."

The case-study students mostly did that at home, relying mainly on their lecture notes and secondarily on their readings. They did not spend much time in the library because they were more comfortable at home.

Rereading either lecture notes or books is by definition revisiting text, but it is not automatically reexposure to *information* because students can note new information each time that they look at a text. For that matter, they could also reexpose themselves to old information the first time they read a text or hear a lecture (e.g., when encountering information already learned in another class). Alternatively, the revisiting of information can be done orally, as when Will played back and transcribed his Biology and Psychology recordings or Greg discussed Statistics and Methods with his classmate Elaine. Working with her provoked all four operations:

Greg: I studied methodology class by talking to Elaine yesterday for two hours at the Midwestern Union.

Investig.: And you said you learned a lot from that. Was it from you talking, explaining something to her or her explaining something to you?

Greg: Both. I had lost my notes a week ago or something, and so she mentioned things in her notes that had slipped my mind and that was a refresher, and then we talked about them, and also by me explaining things that she had questions on, because that solidifies what I do know.

Investig.: You went through her notes? Is that what you did?

Greg: She went through them and was mentioning things; it was all vocal. I didn't really read anything; we went through the book also and we had questions.

However it was done, this kind of reviewing could take place up to four, five, or even more times using different or the same sources. Will, for example, liked to correlate readings with lecture notes with both sitting on his desk. He also tended to review them to see if he had the same ideas when he looked the second time. On rare occasions, though, he could come up with more intensive manipulation-based studying, as I discussed in the section on manipulation.

Greg's integration of manipulation, exposure, and extraction with the focus on anticipated assessments could be simplicity itself; each operation was deployed to see how he could get, remember, and check the content he believed would appear on an exam.

Greg: I remember going through my books, through the chapter before an exam, to remind myself of the topics that I read, then I would try to generalize them. I mean I would try to make them into a more concise form—because that's what you use on a test. They don't ask you to finish the sentence, or to quote something which you read that you might have remembered, a particular sentence that you thought was very succinct. So instead I would go back, and I would try and generalize what they're talking about. Now I'm thinking about physics. I had a physics class, you know. Now they're talking about induction, all right, and then this topic is something else, magnetism, and I would go through and I would refresh myself. It would be visually because I would remember when I would read something on the page, and say, "Oh, that's right; that's the topic, and then this comes next," getting key words. I would look for key words, to refresh that, the material that I read. I wouldn't read it in detail; I would skim through.

Finally, it is important to point out the role of metacognition in studying. In the previous chapter, I mentioned that Greg was rightly skeptical of his sense of understanding. A further example of his sophistication in metacognition can be seen in his awareness of how knowledge structures varied among disciplines and what these variations meant for studying. The following is his comparison of historical concepts with mathematical ones.

Greg: I don't think that I approach [History and Statistics] the same way. When I'm doing the Russian Revolution I am not thinking steps. There are kind of steps to a story; I mean you can stretch the analogy, but the meaning part is essential. It would be futile for me to just memorize a whole bunch of blocks and to try to put them together again and reconstruct the events of the Russian Revolution. If I do not have that blueprint, if I do not understand what they fit into, how they're related to World War I, you know the social conditions going on at the time, people's reasons for doing certain things. You know, why did Czar Nicholas go to the front? You know, why did Lenin have to flee? Why did he come back? If I don't know those, and those are parts of the blueprint, those aren't blocks per se, they're rational—the reasons behind events are the blocks—then I am going to have a real hard time. Whereas in the chi-squared example, the analytical thing, I can get by recognizing a pattern because for me it's easier to recognize patterns with numbers, symbols, which is what statistics is comprised of. But in the Russian Revolution I didn't have any symbols for revolt or for army or for czar. Those have symbols themselves, but for me the word czar has a lot more information tied up with it than X.

The contrast to Will and Sophie could not be more striking. I close with an example of how entirely dependent Sophie was on wording and how she was unable or unwilling to manipulate. "I went over my problems and my homework and stuff, and it was like 'Oh my God!' they were worded all crazy in this outline. They were nothing like the problems and nothing like what we would have in class or on the homework."

Cramming

Because of Greg's irregular attention to his course work, he ended the quarter without much of a grasp of his material in almost all his classes. That meant only one thing: loss of sleep and cramming. He never "pulled an all-nighter"; none of these students did, but Greg did end up getting up at 4 A.M. after going to bed at 11 P.M. several times just before and during finals week. Will also became more intense in his studying right before an exam, but he had been working quite diligently throughout the quarter. Neither Sophie nor Carmin lost any sleep. Carmin even went out the night before her Human Development final to celebrate her birthday, as I mentioned in Chapter 4.

Will spent by far the most hours studying, between six to eight hours and no less than four hours on normal days; Carmin spent the least. The most she put in was three or four hours per day, but often she put in one or two, according to her logs.

DESTINATION

At this point, we have arrived at essentially the same conceptual place as we did in the section on Display in Chapter 7 and that on multiple-choice testing of concepts in Chapter 6. I will not belabor the points made there. Instead, I only want to talk about the way students interacted with the grading process of exams and papers in situations in which they had not performed the other operations adequately. These were cases when they needed to display what they really did not possess.

If we assume the kind of standard approach to academic literacy that I have argued against throughout this study, a student will take a prompt in an exam at face value and so set about answering it. The point being investigated here makes little sense under those circumstances. However, it should be pretty clear by now that to do so is hardly the best way to approach assessments. A strategic approach that looks for incoherencies and so eliminates choices in a multiple-choice item has been shown to be much more successful. Similarly, with exam essay questions, it can be fatal to just take the question at face value rather than use it as a vehicle for display of specific concepts, connections, and/or facts. Note that this specifically academic social motive (Freedman, Adam, and Smart 1994) is confirmed by Professor Tomko in the following complaint about students who do not realize the implicit role of information display in an assessment:

Tomko: This is probably a personal reaction with the students when they write assignments. They don't do it in the way that in a basic sense they are trying to convey to you that they understood and heard the basic material that was sent to them. But they are assuming that because it's in the context of the class, that you know what XittyX is. So they write in the context of the instructor having the knowledge. The purpose of the assignment they don't, I don't know how to convey, the purpose of the assignment is to convey to the instructor that they understood the material as presented to them and read and thought and so on.

Given this purpose, it is worth recalling the case described by Dretske in Chapter 2, and repeated here:

The same phenomenon is illustrated when we "test" a friend about whom we have become suspicious. We ask him to tell us about a situation of which we are already informed. His response tells us (gives us information) about *him*, not about the situation he is (perhaps accurately) describing. (Dretske 1981, p. 117)

If we imagine that the object of Dretske's suspicion is in fact guilty and knows that he is being tested, we arrive at the situation of interest here: an unprepared student who wishes to salvage as many points as possible. Both figures may very well then attempt to give a response that will, they hope, get them off the hook.

Carmin and Greg were fairly successful at getting points they did not feel they really deserved. Greg actually was surprised by his success at this effort in his History course. He felt he had only made a cursory attempt to bamboozle the professor. Before he got his A−, he described his final in the following terms:

Greg: I prepared pretty well for the first question about the Russian Revolution because she is a Russian specialist, I knew it would be on there. That was my guess anyway, and it turned out to be right. I wrote about four pages on that first one and went over the twenty-five-minute time frame, that you might logically draw, and so I had about fifteen minutes for the rest of the hour for the second question, which was World War I. And I didn't answer that very well just because I didn't really know what I was talking about.

However, the instructor seemed to have liked it, had low standards, or was so impressed by the first answer that she was lenient on this one. Possibly Greg's answer was better than he had thought.

Unfortunately, the final was never returned, although Greg left the professor a self-addressed stamped envelope for that purpose. Carmin was less ambivalent about her efforts at what might be called "how to succeed at academics without really trying." One question on the second midterm asked students the following:

(1) Describe the role of schools in fostering development. Describe an ideal school from the social work perspective.

Carmin received nine out of a possible ten points. Note that while the second part of the item appears to open the door to creativity, it also opens it to faking. Carmin chose it for that reason. Looking at her answer, she and I had the following conversation:

Investig.: If you were grading this, would you give it a nine out of ten?
Carmin: No.
Investig.: What would you give it?
Carmin: Maybe a seven.
Investig.: Why?
Carmin: Because it's not very thorough. Even though environment probably explained the ideal school, all I remembered that I'm saying that reading something about the environment, I was not sure exactly what that meant. I was just kind of put it on the page and go with it.
Investig.: You bullshitted.
Carmin: I bullshitted, yeah. I kind of bullshitted on the previous one too.

The previous question Carmin referred to is reproduced as item (2). A key element to successful bullshitting is plausibility, which can be tricky when questions ask for specific points as in this item.

(2) The author discusses poverty and school age children's coping mechanisms. What are three of the authors [*sic*] major ideas in this discussion? What implications does poverty and a youth's coping mechanism have to social work practice?

Note how Carmin was able to attack such an item that called for reference to a book she had barely read, through a combination of sangfroid and common knowledge:

Investig.: Now, the author was Berger.
Carmin: Right.
Investig.: Did you read all of Berger?
Carmin: No.

Investig.: Not even once through?

Carmin: Sometimes no. This particular section, I may have skimmed through, but I didn't read it.

Investig.: You still got a nine out of ten. . . .

Carmin: I thought that was pretty evident why [poverty affects a child]. You don't have as much money, and you can't do as many things. . . . A lot of it is being kind of analytical and taking theories and stuff that I've learned and pretty common knowledge too, I think.

Investig.: Didn't come from the book? Or from . . .

Carmin: Some of it may have, but with how children dress, which is obvious. You get teased. . . . All the kids in our school that were poor, if they were wearing not nice clothes or something, everyone would make fun of them. It's just kind of common knowledge I think.

Yet even when bullshitting fails, all hope is not lost. It is sometime possible to cajole points from a gullible grader:

Sophie: I can remember one thing I really had a problem on. . . . [The final] was over the last couple weeks, and we talked about Stalin and communism and Leninism and all that, and we had to talk about the stages to get to communism. And you had to get from, oh, what's it called, what our society is called, capitalist, you had to go through capitalist, socialist, and then communist. But it was like three or four different phases, and I missed one, and I just couldn't believe that I missed it. And [the TA] pointed it out to me because I asked her and asked her over and over again, and I got at least two points out of her, you know, in asking her. So I . . . I had a B on the final.

Another issue in getting points for minimal effort involves calculating the investment of time and resources. Greg was confused but pleased when he found out that there would be only three questions rather than the five he was expecting on the take-home Changing Family final. Now he could devote more attention elsewhere. Looking for the first time at the final in our interview, he said:

Greg: [talking to the paper] Are you serious? Well, I'll be darned! I was expecting five questions just because, and I'm glad there aren't five questions. Three questions are worth 40%, and now these three questions will be worth 60%, which you know I'm trained to think: "Is it logical?" But, you know, I prefer the questions. It took a long time to write those three questions last time because I didn't read the book. And this time, I didn't read the book either, but she talked about other things in class, and I took notes this time in class, and I have notes to go back to, and I didn't last time.

The most extreme case of this type involved Carmin's Policy course. Carmin put little effort into her final paper because she had doubts that the professor would read it.

Investig.: What grade are you expecting?

Carmin: I wouldn't expect anything lower than a B. Not in that class. I almost don't think he'll read it. It's one professor with sixty students that are writing nine- to twelve-page papers. . . .

Investig.: No TA.

Carmin: No. And I know for the midterm, I don't know if he read those for sure.

Investig.: How did he grade them if he didn't read them?

Carmin: I don't know. Everybody that I saw got a hundred. [laughs]

Investig.: If you're not gonna read them, and you have to justify grades, better to put on a high grade.

Carmin: Also, a girl that's in the social work classes right now knows someone from the previous year's class, and they said that in writing their final paper, they wrote something in the middle totally bizarre like asking about chocolate chip cookies and writing like different types of chocolate chip cookies and handed back the paper, and there wasn't any comment next to that. So I kind of don't think that he's reading them.

She received an A in the class, and the paper itself was not returned.

Although the cases like the last example may seem to be inappropriate to consider in a study of academic literacy because they show the system going awry, such academic horror stories are unfortunately not that unusual. A realistic account of students' academic experience has little reason, other than distaste, to leave them out of an analysis of how students function in college. I am sure that if readers reflect on their own histories, it will not be hard to find similar cases. I myself recall handing in a paper that I had made little effort on because I was sure that the professor would not read it, and considering the grade I got, I too was correct in my calculations. It is a virtue of the analysis of academic literacy as a game that it can accommodate such instances. In the end in this case, like the more normal cases, Carmin took information from a variety of sources, processed it various ways, and eventually displayed it. She just put little effort into it just as a player with a nearly guaranteed win puts little effort into achieving a score. In fact, one area not examined in this study because it just did not come up might be how students strategically select courses and professors that they expect will call for little effort in order to get high grades and devote more time and energy to more difficult classes. That too is a possible strategic decision.

SUMMARY

In this chapter, I dealt largely with issues that escaped attention in the focus on information types and operations in previous chapters. In so doing, I hope to have contextualized those elements of the game in the context of actual play and to have dispelled some of the sense (always a danger with abstract constructs) that the two sets of categories are somehow not part of real life.

What stands out in this analysis—what it maintained from the previous two chapters—is the strategic nature of the students' approaches to their courses. The strategies involved are not really learning strategies or even study strategies as they are generally understood in the literature. Those kinds of strategies may play a role, but when they do, they are invariably subsumed in what is in truth an overall game plan designed to maximize a score.

NOTES

1. The data gathering took place just before the boom in electronic communication in course materials.

2. He did not acknowledge this in our sessions, but it appears to be the only plausible explanation.

3. I take this requirement as evidence of a contest of wills between the instructor and students over the textbook reading. Sophie was probably not alone in finding the origins and modus operandi of the *Partido Revolucionario Institucional* less than compelling reading.

4. Note that she is aware of the misspelling and indicates it with a circled "sp." She does not do so with the equally invented spelling of Allende or Chile.

PART III

FINAL

The final part of this book contains only one short chapter. In general, the ideas put forward constitute the short version of my answer to the original questions I asked myself as a teacher of developmental college students. The long version can be found in Part II.

These answers are the result of a brief period of data gathering and a long period of data analysis, reviewing more and more literature, and a lot of reflection. In part the reason that it took so long was that I had to come to a counterintuitive conclusion that has at most found only echoes in undercurrents in the literature, and use that as my starting point for analysis. I found I could only arrive at an answer by considering academic literacy as a phenomenon in its own right, not as a form of socialization, a function of cognitive skills, or the result of linguistic competencies. Nor were barriers to academic literacy mere artifacts of discrimination, inappropriate assessments, mechanisms for social reproduction, or vacuous literacy norms. Success in college, I found, was, *related* to all these factors, identified in so much research on academic literacy over the past few decades, but it was more than just them. It was a system, cocreated by all its human participants to accomplish a variety of sometimes conflicting social purposes. As such, it is interesting in its own right and worth making the effort to understand. In what follows I lay out my conclusions about this system, describe its ideological implications, and make some pedagogical suggestions that arise from this view.

Chapter 9

Conclusions

WHAT IT TAKES TO SUCCEED IN COLLEGE

If I had to reduce what I learned from doing this research into a few paragraphs, I would say the following. For a student, academics in college is a multifaceted game-like activity that is best played only after learning as many of the rules, strategies, and principles governing it as possible. Although each class constitutes its own instantiation of this game, and no two such games will be identical, all share the same basic Design. In each game, students are players who (1) are given access to some information, though this may be very abstract; (2) some guidance as to what to do with it; and (3) mechanisms to display it for points. Their task is to first figure out what the target information is for that game—including which of the six types it takes—and how best to get it to the display using the four operations. The next is to implement collection and channeling of the course content to the assigned displays. In doing so, they need to determine what information is available where, what they may already have before beginning, and how the different forms of information are most efficiently processed. The final task is to display the information needed in such a way that the grader will recognize it.

After end-game displays are presented, scores will be given in response. Sometimes the scoring will be objective, in the sense that it will be based on matching preestablished targets, as on multiple-choice items. Other times, it will be based on a more slippery rubric, not unlike how judges at acrobatic events hand out ratings based on various criteria, as on a written assignment. Such rubrics need to be anticipated and satisfied, even though they may include abstract metainformational objectives that are never stated. Across games, scoring is somewhat inconsistent not only with regards to information that is rewarded, but also in terms of rigor, and the same can be said for the amount of guidance and support provided by faculty.

It is the variation between games, the existence of multiple methods of information finding, movement, and display, and the sometimes subjective scoring that account for the ill structure of academic literacy. Yet within this ill structure, there are certain principles that remain constant—such as those discussed in the last few chapters—and these can be learned. Knowing that overall structure and the various common patterns and tactics will lead to high scores because they constitute tools for more skillful play. Still, as in any game, there is no guarantee for success; therein lies the challenge.

Social and Political Implications

The most striking limitation of this view is the omission of the primary reasons we would like to think colleges exist: to provide a forum in which people learn and conduct research. Instead, it focuses on the crass results of the efforts of faculty and institutions to compel students to do the work we think is good for them. The academic achievement game, as I have explicated in the study, is in the end the students' way of constructing and responding to those demands.

As such, the view I espouse can be seen as a doubly pessimistic one. On the one hand, it makes clear some of the main flaws in the system. On the other, it argues that those flaws are inherent in the design of academic literacy and cannot be changed without the university changing beyond recognition. I expect that this vision will be particularly unattractive to those espousing critical-theoretic views of education because of the affinity of this trend for breaking down hegemonic structures. However, from the pragmatist's perspective, compromise and imperfections are the way of the world; it is our obligation only to do the best we can with them. Also, as pragmatists never seem to tire of pointing out, great evil has been done in the name of idealism. Admittedly, the roads to any number of educational hells have not only been paved with good intentions—some pretty selfish asphalt can be found there too—but educational idealism has sometimes cleared the path for the steamrollers. Metaphors aside, we can only make reforms starting with a realistic understanding of where we currently are at. I hope to have begun to provide a realistic sense of what one aspect of college is for students here and now.

After all, despite the efforts of reformers ranging from Dewey to the Chinese Red Guards to the Brown University trustees to Greg, all of whom wished in their different ways and on different scales to bring it down, this design has shown a remarkable resilience. It has always sprung back to life in each case. If the game is inevitable, it may be because it is the most logical way to organize learning in large-scale settings and to find a way of balancing the interests of various stakeholders in the process.

Furthermore, if learning has not been the center of the study, that is not because none took place. Although it is true that the student participants seemed to believe that the achievement game got in the way of their learning, it is equally the case that without having played it, they would have learned a lot less. Each respondent was interested in learning, and each thought they learned a lot in college, perhaps not as much as they would have hoped, but a lot. None wished to drop out or to cynically only continue to get the credential. Therefore, while I have not examined learning, that subject has been the focus of many other studies, and I believe it is time to look at another, admittedly less high-minded, aspect of college; however, it is one that is interesting and important for all that.

I have also backgrounded political influences on the system, again not because I believe that they are unimportant but because their role in the game was generally indirect, and in any case they have also received considerable attention in the literature. Still, I do want to acknowledge them here, if only because their role was visible even given the relative cultural homogeneity of the research participants. There is good evidence, for example, that Will's socioeconomic and educational background was a major reason that he lacked the knowledge that the other students had. Similarly, different forms of unfairness associated with gender and family lie behind Sophie's travails, even some of those that she exacerbated by her own behavior. Finally, gender issues very nearly pushed Carmin into a traditionally female field for which she was ill-suited. The teaching she received may also have suffered from the gendered status of social work generally and its marginalization from the interests of privileged segments of society. Certainly, at least two of Carmin's classes appeared to be plagued by depressingly low expectations combined with dubious professionalism in instruction. By contrast, traditionally masculine areas such as the sciences, from which Carmin was discouraged from entering, were characterized by a certain academic social Darwinism, from which Will and perhaps also Sophie suffered. Only Greg seemed to be entirely privileged by his background, and yet ironically he was the only one who clearly saw how that privilege impacted on his career. Interestingly, he was also the only one determined to reject it, but in doing so he lashed out in ways that made him uncomfortable and which ultimately failed to make the changes he was seeking.

Still, the relative homogeneity and status of the respondents as European American Midwesterners limits the applicability of the study to some degree. Although I believe the game I have described is universal, I need to emphasize that I make no such claims for particular ways of playing it that I have looked at here (i.e., the actual findings of the study rather than its framework). I have only looked at four students in a single university over the course of eleven weeks. Had I looked at them during a different quarter, much would have been different. Had I examined four other students of similar backgrounds, there would have been greater differences. Had I examined Latino, African American, or international students, there would have been other still more profound variations. The same could be said if I had looked at students in a different university, one with semesters rather than quarters, with a different population, with a different mission, or in a different country (see Newman, Trenchs, and Pujol, under review).

So I do not wish to deny the importance of culture and institutional politics. Sometimes these types of differences can be obvious; in Italy and Argentina universities rely on oral rather than written exams, for example, and students there may never encounter a research paper. In Spain, course failure and repetition are common, while attendance in class can be sporadic. In Vietnam, students use far more of their own initiative to manage without access to many written materials in English; in some institutions in that country, I am told, students bribe teachers for greater attention and even sometimes for grades themselves. Yet in each place, students are all recognizably playing the same game. They are provided with some kind of information source and they use it to create some kind of display for which they are rewarded (variously) or punished.

Pedagogy

There is an unfortunate tendency to assume that accounting for educational phenomena and developing pedagogies based on those understandings is a zero-sum game and that one proposed cause or theoretical depiction necessarily precludes another. As a result, we find beliefs that are thought to be incompatible without there being any real logical or evidential contradictions: Children are said to learn to read by phonics *or* by top-down schema completion. Becoming competent in a second language is claimed to be social learn-ing *or* it is internal acquisition. These are false disjunctions, made even worse sometimes when politics gets in the way. For example, when the fact that an ideological opponent takes an educational policy position becomes reason enough to oppose it. When the stakes are so high, eclecticism and pragmatism can be derided as equiva-lent to being unprincipled.

What I propose instead is a principled eclecticism. Within the limitations of the game-like system described, this study points to possible ways to improve the students' experiences. The basis for such hopes can be found in the comments made by the four re-search subjects and their experience. It had been a difficult quarter for all four of them in different ways. Greg had seen his frustra-tions with college and his family come to a head, and worse, his attempt to resolve them frustrated. Carmin had felt the need to change majors and therefore universities because of her academic dissatisfaction. Sophie had endured taking two classes she was uninterested in because of the lack of financial support coming from her family and MSU requirements, and she knew it would be a long time before she could graduate or even enter her preferred program. Will found his hopes for graduate school and his self-image dealt a further blow in the form of continuing low grades.

Yet there were no sad endings. Far from letting herself be a vic-tim, Carmin had used her own initiative to take up a more rigorous major that she was excited by. Even Sophie was somewhat closer to finishing her hated general education requirements and so was moving toward her major, which she *was* interested in. For Will the university had propelled him toward a professional future that he only set out for himself relatively late in adolescence, and in so doing was fulfilling its promise to be a route to economic progress. Greg similarly made his peace with the university. After a year off working, he decided to pursue a M.S.W. degree, and as part of that program ended up, ironically, advising undergraduates. As this book goes to press, he is beginning his professional career.

Furthermore, all were glad they participated in the research; all felt they had learned more about what they were doing in college. Will even stopped by my office a couple of quarters later to say how much he appreciated what he had learned by participating. He re-ported that he was no longer struggling, and although he had given up his efforts to be a psychologist (he had switched to a business major) he was now getting an A– average. Also, he was no longer killing himself with effort. I would like to think that the kind of experience that participating in the research provided for these students is one reason that these improvements took place. I have lost track of Carmin, but in her closing interview she also remarked how being asked the questions made her think about what she was doing as she studied, rather than just taking the experience at face value. In this way, she became more aware of the elements involved in what she was doing, and so gained more control over them.

Any program coming out of this research would build upon these kinds of positive foundations to advance students' understanding. It might seem Pollyannaish to say so in this age of the exuberant gloom of postmodernism, but every university despite its flaws presents opportunities to its students. That promise is why it is worth going to the effort to describe the design of academic achievement in a theoretically rigorous way, even if doing so shows limitations and flaws in the system that cannot be entirely repaired. It is also why it is worth building a pedagogy that can extend the promise to more students. Just as it happened with the research participants, doing so means increasing students' awareness of the system in which they must learn and receive credentials. Realism is not pessimism.

The Multiliteracies framework on which this study is based points the way to fomenting this kind of greater awareness. It involves including an explicated design as the content of a literacy curriculum. In a Multiliteracies pedagogy (Cope and Kalantzis 2000b), that would consist of four (not necessarily sequential) components:

1. Situated practice: a form of immersion in practice.
2. Overt instruction: encouraging conscious reflection.
3. Critical framing: interpreting of social and cultural contexts of practice.
4. Transformed practice: a shifting of contexts of use.

Using the Design of the game as the content of an academic literacy program means that Design elements can be iterated in a different way in each component. Following this plan, such a pedagogy would first encourage practice of the various elements in the achievement game, either as part of a literacy class or as reflective practice in regular classes. Second, it would aim to make students conscious of the Design elements, including the differences between grades and learning, the four types of information, and the six types of operations. Third, it would invite students to understand why the game exists and how it is played by different individuals. Finally, it would show how the context of the class affects the game, and more important, how students can appropriate or *master* the game for their own purposes. On this point, the idea is to make the game serve their purposes in both learning and in achieving.

In any case, using Design as a focal content in a pedagogy should be the next step in developing our understanding of academic literacy. It is an important next step because of the tendency for pedagogical paradigms to be applied prematurely, before they have undergone thorough validation via research. Such research would surely come up with refinements or perhaps substantial modifications to the understanding of what students do and how they achieve what I have found here. It will be interesting to see how they can be extended and how they will need to be modified.

That limitation acknowledged, I believe that it is also possible to extend the insights developed here into other areas. When Wittgenstein described communicative systems in terms of a game, he was making just that kind of general claim. The same could be said for design. Surely other domains of communication and literacy also have the kinds of flexible structuring that obey their social motives and practical requirements. It would be interesting to explore the extent to which any or all of the six information types identified here can be found in business, artistic communities of practice, or other areas where rewards flow from information displays. Similarly, what operations on information are performed in these areas? All this is open to exploration, explication, and perhaps teaching. After all, not only success in college or how to get rich are ill-structured problems. Successfully communicating in every domain from love to war is just that. What are these games like?

References

Alexander, P. A., and F. Dochy. 1994. Adults' views about knowing and believing. In *Beliefs about text and instruction with text*, ed. R. Garner and P. A. Alexander, pp. 224–244. Hillsdale, N.J.: Erlbaum.

Anderson, T. H., and B. B. Armbruster. 1984. Studying. In *The handbook of reading research*, ed. P. D. Pearson, pp. 657–679. London: Longman.

Barlow, M. 1992. *A situated theory of agreement*. New York: Garland.

Bartholomae, D., and A. Petrosky. 1988. *Facts, artifacts, and counterfacts: Theory and method for a reading and writing course*. Upper Montclair, N.J.: Boynton-Cook.

Bartsch, R. 1987. *Norms of language*. New York: Longman.

Barwise, J. 1986/1988. Information and circumstance in Jon Barwise. In *The Situation in Logic*. CSLI Lecture Notes 17. Stanford, Calif.: Center for the Study of Language and Information. First published in *Notre Dame Journal of Formal Logic* 27: 324–338.

Barwise, J., and J. Echemendy. 1990. Visual information and valid reasoning. In *Visualization in mathematics*, ed. W. Zimmerman, pp. 9–24. Washington, D.C.: Mathematical Association of America.

Barwise, J., and J. Perry. 1983. *Situations and attitudes*. Cambridge, Mass.: MIT Press.

Becker, H., B. Geer, and E. C. Hughes. 1968. *The academic side of college life*. New York: Wiley.

Benesch, S. 1995. Genres and processes in a sociocultural context. *Journal of Second Language Writing* 4 (2): 191–195.

Berkenkotter, C., and T. N. Huckin. 1995. *Genre knowledge in disciplinary communities*. Hillsdale, N.J.: Erlbaum.

Block, E. 1986. The comprehension strategies of second language readers. *TESOL Quarterly* 20: 463–494.

Boekaerts, M. 1995. Self-regulated learning: Bridging the gap between metacognitive and metamotivation theories. *Educational Psychologist* 30 (4): 195–200.

Bogdan, R. C., and S. K. Biklen. 1998. *Qualitative research for education: An introduction to theory and methods.* Newton, Mass.: Allyn & Bacon.

Briggs, C. L., and R. Baumann. 1992. Genre, intertextuality, and social power. *Journal of Linguistic Anthropology* 2: 131–172.

Brown, J. S., A. Collins, and P. Duguid. 1989. Situated cognition and the culture of learning. *Educational Researcher* 18: 32–42.

Carson, J. G., N. D. Chase, S. U. Gibson, and M. F. Hargrove. 1992. Literacy demands of the undergraduate curriculum. *Reading Research and Instruction* 31 (4): 25–50.

Cazden, C. B. 1988. *Classroom discourse.* Portsmouth, N.H.: Heinemann/ Boynton-Cook.

Chimbganda, A. B. 2000. Communication strategies used in the writing of answers in biology by ESL first year science students of the University of Botswana. *English for Specific Purposes* 19: 305–329.

Chiseri-Strater, E. 1991. *Academic literacies: The public and private discourse of university students.* Portsmouth, N.H.: Heinemann/Boynton-Cook.

Cope, B., and M. Kalantzis. 2000a. Designs for social futures. In *Multiliteracies: Literacy learning and the design of social futures*, ed. B. Cope and M. Kalantzis, pp. 203–234. London and New York: Routledge.

Cope, B., and M. Kalantzis. 2000b. *Multiliteracies: Literacy learning and the design of social futures.* London and New York: Routledge.

Crooks, T. J. 1988. The impact of classroom evaluation practices on students. *Review of Educational Research* 58 (4): 438–481.

Delpit, L. 1995. *Other people's children: Cultural conflict in the classroom.* New York: New Press.

Devlin, K. 1991. *Logic and information.* Cambridge, U.K.: Cambridge University Press.

Devlin, K. 1997. *Goodbye Descartes: The end of logic and the search for a new cosmology of the mind.* New York: John Wiley.

Devlin, K., and D. Rosenberg. 1996. *Language at work: Analyzing communication breakdown in the workplace to inform system design.* CSLI Lecture Notes 66. Stanford, Calif.: Center for the Study of Language and Information.

Dretske, F. 1981. *Knowledge and the flow of information.* Cambridge, Mass.: Bradford Books/MIT Press.

Dunston, P. 1992. A critique of graphic organizer research. *Reading Research and Instruction* 31 (2): 57–65.

Entwistle, N. 1984. Contrasting perspectives on learning. In *The experience of learning*, ed. F. Marton, D. Hounsell, and N. Entwistle, pp. 1–18. Edinburgh: Scottish Academic Press.

Entwistle, N. 1987. A model of the teaching–learning process. In *Student learning: Research in education and cognitive psychology*, ed. J.T.E. Richardson, M. W. Eysenck, and D. W. Piper, pp. 13–28. Philadelphia and Milton Keynes, U.K.: Society for Reseach into Higher Education/Open University Press.

Erickson, F. 1986. Qualitative methods in research on teaching. In *Handbook of research on teaching*, ed. M. C. Wittrock, pp. 119–161. New York: Macmillan.

Flower, L. 1989. Negotiating academic discourse (Reading-to-Write Report No. 10). Technical Report No. 29. Washington, D.C.: Office of Educational Research and Improvement (ED 306600).

Freedman, A., C. Adam, and G. Smart. 1994. Wearing suits to class: Simulating genres and simulations as genre. *Written Communication* 11: 193–226.

Freedman, A., and P. Medway. 1994. Introduction. In *Learning and teaching genre*, ed. A. Freedman and P. Medway, pp. 1–22. Portsmouth, N.H.: Heinemann/Boynton-Cook.

Gee, J. P. 1989. Literacy, discourse, and linguistics: Introduction. *Journal of Education* 171: 5–25.

Gee, J. P. 1991. *Social linguistics and literacies*. London: Falmer.

Gee, J. P. 2000. New people in new worlds: Networks, the new capitalism and schools. in *Multiliteracies: Literacy learning and the design of social futures*, ed. B. Cope and M. Kalantzis, pp. 43–68. London and New York: Routledge.

Geisler, C. 1994. *Academic literacy and the nature of expertise*. Hillsdale, N.J.: Erlbaum.

Goody, J., and I. Watt. 1968. The consequences of literacy. In *Literacy in traditional societies*, ed. J. Goody, pp. 27–68. Cambridge, U.K. and New York: Cambridge University Press.

Gordon, C. M., and D. Hanauer. 1995. The interaction between task and meaning construction in EFL reading comprehension tests. *TESOL Quarterly* 29: 299–324.

Greene, S. 1993. The role of task in the development of academic thinking through reading and writing in a college history course. *Research in the Teaching of English* 27: 46–75.

Greeno, J. G., and J. L. Moore. 1993. Situativity and symbols: Response to Vera and Simon. *Cognitive Science* 17: 49–59.

Haas, C. 1994. Learning to read biology: One student's rhetorical development in college. *Written Communication* 11: 43–84.

Hambleton, R. K. 1989. Introduction to a special issue on item response theory. *International Journal of Educational Research* 13 (2): 123–125.

Hammer, D. 1994. Epistemological beliefs in introductory physics. *Cognition and Instruction* 12 (2): 151–183.

Hasan, R. 1998. The disempowerment game: Bourdieu and language in literacy. *Linguistics and Education* 10 (1): 25–87.

Heath, S. B. 1982. What no bedtime story means: Narrative skills at home and in school. *Language in Society* 11: 49–76.

Heath, S. B. 1983. *Ways with words: Language, life, and work in communities and classrooms*. Cambridge, U.K. and New York: Cambridge University Press.

Hiebert, J., and P. Lefevre. 1986. Conceptual and procedural knowledge in mathematics: An introductory analysis. In *Conceptual and procedural knowledge: The case of mathematics*, ed. J. Hiebert, pp. 1–27. Hillsdale, N.J.: Erlbaum.

Hill, C. 1992. Testing and assessment: An ecological approach. Inaugural lecture for the Arthur I. Gates chair in language and education. New York: Teachers College, Columbia University.

Hill, C. 1995. Testing and assessment: An applied linguistics perspective. *Educational Assessment* 2: 179–212.

Hill, C. 2000. Linguistic and cultural diversity: A growing challenge to American higher education. Paper given at the College Board, New York.

Hill, C., and E. Larsen. 2000. *Children and reading tests*. Stamford, Conn.: Ablex.

Hill, C., and K. Parry. 1989. Autonomous and pragmatic models of literacy: Reading assessment in adult education. *Linguistics and Education* 1 (3): 233–283.

Hill, C., and K. Parry. 1992. The test at the gate: Models of literacy in reading assessment. *TESOL Quarterly* 26 (3): 433–461.

Hill, C., and K. Parry. 1994. Models of literacy: The nature of reading tests. In *From testing to assessment: English as an international language*, ed. C. Hill and K. Parry, pp. 665–692. New York: Longman.

Hirsch, E. D. 1988. *Cultural literacy: What every American needs to know.* New York: Vintage Books.

Horowitz, D. M. 1986. What professors actually require: Academic tasks for the ESL classroom. *TESOL Quarterly* 20: 445–462.

Hounsell, D. 1984. Learning and essay-writing. In *The experience of learning*, ed. F. Marton, D. Hounsell, and N. Entwistle, pp. 103–123. Edinburgh: Scottish Academic Press.

Hynd, C. R., and S. A. Stahl. 1998. What do we mean by knowledge and learning? In *Learning from text across conceptual domains*, ed. C. Hynd, S. A. Stahl, M. Carr, and S. M. Glynn, pp. 15–44. Mahwah, N.J.: Erlbaum.

Israel, D., and J. Perry. 1991. Information and architecture. In *Situation theory and its applications, V2*, ed. J. Barwise, J. M. Gawron, G. Plotkin, and S. Tutiya, pp. 147–159. CSLI Lecture Notes No. 26. Stanford, Calif.: Center for the Study of Language and Information.

Johansson, M., and C. Jonsson. 1996. Higher education and study cultures: a comparison between students at Umea University, Sweden and at the University of Wisconsin, Madison. Paper presented at the annual conference of the American Educational Research Association, April 8–12, New York.

Johns, A. M. 1981. Necessary English: A faculty survey. *TESOL Quarterly* 15: 51–58.

Johns, A. M. 1991. Interpreting an English competency exam: The frustrations of an ESL science student. *Written Communication* 8: 379–401.

Johns, A. M. 1997. *Text, role and context*. Cambridge, U.K.: Cambridge University Press.

Kress, G. 2000. Design and transformation: New theories of meaning. In *Multiliteracies: Literacy learning and the design of social futures*, ed. B. Cope and M. Kalantzis, pp. 153–161. London and New York: Routledge.

Kruglanski, A. W. 1989. *Lay epistemics and human knowledge: Cognitive and motivational bases.* New York: Plenum Press.

Kruglanski, A. W. 1990. Lay epistemic theory in social–cognitive psychology. *Psychological Inquiry* 1 (3): 181–197.

Langer, J. 1992. Speaking of knowing: Conceptions of understanding in the academic disciplines. In *Writing, teaching, and learning in the disciplines*, ed. A. Herrington and C. Moran, pp. 69–85. New York: Modern Language Association.

Laurillard, D. 1984. Learning from problem solving. In *The experience of learning*, ed. F. Marton, D. Hounsell, and N. Entwistle, pp. 124–143. Edinburgh: Scottish Academic Press.

Laurillard, D. 1987. The different forms of learning in psychology and education. In *Student learning: Research in education and cognitive psychology*, ed. J.T.E. Richardson, M. W. Eysenck, and D. W. Piper, pp. 198–207. Philadelphia and Milton Keynes, U.K.: Society for Research into Higher Education/Open University Press.

Lave, J., and E. Wenger. 1991. *Situated learning: Legitimate peripheral participation.* New York: Cambridge University Press.

Leki, I. 1995. Coping strategies of ESL students in writing tasks across the curriculum. *TESOL Quarterly* 29 (2): 235–260.

Luria, A. R. 1974/1976. *Cognitive development: Its cultural and social foundations.* Translated by M. L. Morillas and L. Solotaroff. Cambridge, Mass.: Harvard University Press.

Mann, S. 2000. The student's experience of reading. *Higher Education* 39: 297–317.

Marton, F., and R. Säljö. 1976. On qualitative differences in learning, outcome, and process. *British Journal of Educational Psychology* 46: 4–11.

Mehan, H. 1980. The competent student. *Anthropology in Education Quarterly* 11: 131–152.

Merriam, S. B. 1988. *Case study research in education: A qualitative approach.* San Francisco: Jossey-Bass.

Miller, C. M., and M. R. Parlett. 1974. *Up to the mark: A study of the examination game.* Guildford: Society for Research into Higher Education.

Moffatt, M. 1991. *Coming of age in New Jersey.* New Brunswick, N.J.: Rutgers University Press.

Nelson, J. 1990. This was an easy assignment: Examining how students interpret academic writing tasks. *Research in the Teaching of English* 24: 362–396.

New London Group. 1996/2000. A pedagogy of multiliteracies: Designing social futures. In *Multiliteracies: Literacy learning and the design of social futures*, ed. B. Cope and M. Kalantzis, pp. 9–37. London and New York: Routledge. First published in *Harvard Educational Review* 66: 60–92.

Newman, M. 1996. Correctness and its conceptions. *Journal of Basic Writing* 5: 1.

Newman, M. 1997. *Epicene pronouns: The linguistics of a prescriptive problem.* New York: Garland.

Newman, M. 1998. What can pronouns tell us: A case study of English epicenes. *Studies in Language* 22 (2): 353–389.

Newman, M. 2001. The academic literacy game: The Design of academic achievement. *Written Communication* 18 (4): 470–505.

Newman, M. Forthcoming. Definitions of literacy and their consequences. In *The language reader*, ed. T. Smoke, H. Luria, and D. Seymore. New York: Harcourt Brace.

Newman, M., M. Trenchs, and M. Pujol. Under review. Core academic literacy principles versus culture-specific practices: A multi-case study of academic achievement. *English for Specific Purposes.*

Nist, S. L., M. L. Simpson, S. Olejnik, and D. L. Mealey. 1991. The relation between self-selected study processes and test performance. *American Educational Research Journal* 28 (4): 849–874.

Nolen, S. B. 1988. Reasons for studying: Motivational orientations and study strategies. *Cognition and Instruction* 5 (4): 269–287.

Norman, D. 1993. *Things that make us smart.* Reading, Mass.: Addison-Wesley.

Norman, D. A. 1990. Cognitive artifacts. In *Designing interaction: Psychology at the human-computer interface*, ed. J. M. Carroll, pp. 17–38. New York: Cambridge University Press.

Ong, W. J. 1992. Writing is a technology that restructures thought. In *The lingusitics of literacy*, ed. P. Downing, S. Lima, and M. Noonan. Philadelphia and Amsterdam: Benjamins.

Pennycook, A. 1996. Borrowing others' words: Text, ownership, memory, and plagiarism. *TESOL Quarterly* 30: 201–230.

Peterson, S. E. 1992. The cognitive functions of underlining as a study technique. *Reading Research and Instruction* 31 (2): 49–56.

Pintrich, P. R., and T. Garcia. 1991. Student goal orientation and self-regulation in the college clasroom. *Advances in Motivation and Achievement* 7: 371–402.

Pintrich, P. R., and T. Garcia. 1994. Self-regulated learning in college students: Knowledge, strategies, and motivation. In *Student motivation, cognition, and learning: Essays in honor of Wilbert J. McKeachie*, ed. P. R. Pintrich, D. R. Brown, and C. E. Weinstein, pp. 113–133.

Pintrich, P. R., R. W. Marx, and R. A. Boyle. 1993. Beyond cold conceptual change: The role of motivational beliefs and classroom contextual factors in the process of conceptual change. *Review of Educational Research* 63 (2): 167–199.

Pintrich, P. R., and B. Shrauben. 1992. Students' motivational beliefs and their cognitive engagement in classroom academic tasks. In *Student perceptions in the classroom*, ed. D. H. Schunk and J. L. Meece, pp. 149–183. Mahwah, N.J.: Erlbaum.

Pollard, C., and I. Sag. 1994. *Head-driven phrase structure grammar.* Stanford, Calif.: Center for the Study of Language and Information; Chicago: University of Chicago Press.

Poole, D. 1994. Routine testing practices and the linguistic construction of knowledge. *Cognition and Instruction* 12 (2): 125–150.

Raimes, A. 1985. What unskilled ESL students do as they write: A classroom study of composing. *TESOL Quarterly* 19 (2): 229–258.

Ramanathan, V., and D. Atkinson. 1999. Individualism, academic writiing, and ESL writers. *Journal of Second Language Writing* 8 (1): 45–75.

Robinson, W. P., and C. A. Tayler. 1989. Correlates of low academic attainment in three countries. *International Journal of Educational Research* 13: 581–595.

Rumelhart, D. E., and D. E. Norman. 1988. Representation in memory. In *Stevens' handbook of experimental psychology*, ed. R. C. Atkinson, R. J. Herrnstein, G. Lindzey, and R. E. Luce, pp. 511–582. New York: Wiley.

Schallert, D. L., P. A. Alexander, and E. T. Goetz. 1988. Implicit instruction of strategies for learning from text. In *Learning and study strategies: Issues in assessment, instruction, and evaluation*, ed. C. E. Weinstein, E. T. Goetz, and P. A. Alexander, pp. 193–214. San Diego: Academic Press.

Schommer, M. 1994. An emerging conceptualization of epistemological beliefs and their role in learning. In *Beliefs about text and instruction with text*, ed. R. Garner and P. A. Alexander, pp. 25–40. Hillsdale, N.J.: Erlbaum.

Schutz, P. A. 1994. Goals as transactive point beween motivation and cognition. In *Student motivation, cognition, and learning: Essays in honor of Wilbert J. McKeachie*, ed. P. R. Pintrich, D. R. Brown, and C. E. Weinstein, pp. 135–156. Hillsdale, N.J.: Erlbaum.

Scollon, R. 1995. Plagiarism and ideology: Identity in intercultural discourse. *Language in Society* 24 (1): 1–28.

Scribner, S., and M. Cole. 1981. *The psychology of literacy*. Cambridge, Mass.: Harvard University Press.

Shannon, C. E. 1949. *The mathematical theory of information*. Urbana: University of Illinois Press.

Simpson, S. G., and G. Nist. 1997. Perspectives on learning history: A case study. *Journal of Literacy Research* 29 (3): 363–395.

Snow, C. E., and D. K. Dickinson. 1991. Skills that aren't basic in a new conception of literacy. In *Literate systems and individual lives: Perspectives on literacy and schooling*, ed. E. M. Jennings and A. C. Purves, pp. 179–191. Albany: State University of New York Press.

Spack, R. 1997. The acquisition of academic literacy in a second language: A longitudinal case study. *Written Communication* 14: 3–62.

Steinberg, I., G. Bohning, and F. Choning. 1991. Comprehension monitoring strategies of nonproficient college readers. *Reading Research and Instruction* 30 (3): 63–75.

Street, B. 1984. *Literacy in theory and practice*. New York: Cambridge University Press.

Street, B. V. 1993. The new literacy studies. In *Crosscultural approaches to literacy*, ed. B. Street, pp. 1–21. Cambridge and New York: Cambridge University Press.

Street, B. V. 1995. *Social literacies: Critical approaches to literacy in development, ethnography, and education*. London and New York: Longman.

Swales, J. M. 1990. *Genre analysis: English in academic research settings.* New York: Cambridge University Press.

Thomas, J. W., and W. D. Rower. 1986. Academic studying: The role of learning strategies. *Educational Psychologist* 21: 19–41.

Thorkildsen, T. A., and J. G. Nicholls. 1991. Students' critiques as motivation. *Educational Psychologist* 26: 347–368.

Treisman, U. 1992. Studying students studying calculus: A look at the lives of minority mathematics students in college. *The College Mathematics Journal* 23: 362–372.

Trimbur, J. 1994. Taking the social turn: Teaching writing post-process. *College Composition and Communication* 45: 108–118.

Van Meter, P., L. Yokoi, and M. Pressley. 1994. College students' theory of note-taking derived from their perceptions of note-taking. *Journal of Educational Psychology* 86 (3): 323–338.

Vera, A. H., and H. A. Simon. 1993. Situated action: A symbolic interpretation. *Cognitive Science* 17: 7–48.

Walters, K. S. 1990. Critical thinking, rationality, and the vulcanization of students. *Journal of Higher Education* 61: 448–467.

Walvoord, B. E., and L. P. McCarthy. 1990. *Thinking and writing in College: A naturalistic study of students in four disciplines.* Urbana, Ill.: National Council of Teachers of English.

Weinstein, C., and D. Meyer. 1986. The teaching of learning strategies. In *Handbook of research on teaching*, 3d ed., ed. M. C. Wittrock, pp. 315–327. New York: Collier.

Weinstein, C. E., and D. K. Meyer. 1991. Cognitive learning strategies and college teaching. In *College teaching: From theory to practice*, ed. R. J. Menges and M. D. Svinicki, pp. 15–26. San Francisco: Jossey-Bass.

Wineburg, S. 1997. Beyond "breadth and depth": Subject matter knowledge and assessment. *Theory into Practice* 36: 255–261.

Wittgenstein, L. 1953. *Philosophical investigations.* New York: Macmillan.

Wittgenstein, L. 1963. *On certainty.* New York: Macmillan.

Zhang, J., and D. A. Norman. 1994. Representations in distributed cognitive tasks. *Cognitive Science* 18: 87–122.

Index

Freedman, A., 8, 12, 20–22

Gee, J. P., 8
Genre, 13, 20–25, 28, 33, 106, 108, 110
Grades, 4, 6, 8, 10, 13, 59, 61–66
Grading systems, 5, 61, 62, 63, 64

Infons, 69, 70, 75, 76, 83, 139, 140, 141
Informational structure, 67, 96
Information flow, 15, 59
Information theory, 23, 26
Information types, 41, 42, 67, 68, 71, 73, 91, 100, 113, 115, 117, 119, 123, 125

Johns, A., 6, 9, 20, 21, 32, 33

Kalantzis, M., 7, 8
Kress, G., 7, 20, 34

Language games, 8
Laurillard, D., 16–19, 21
Learning, 13, 14, 16–21, 24, 59, 60, 62–64, 66
Learning strategies, 14
Learning versus memorization, 69
Lectures, 118, 119, 124, 129, 135

Motivation, 63, 121, 137
Multiliteracies, 7, 8, 87, 174
Multiple choice, 53, 72, 94, 135, 136, 138, 141, 142, 169

Naturalistic pedagogy, 98
New London Group, 87
Norman, D., 67
Norms, 6, 7
Norms of communication, 105
Norms of writing, 106

Operation, 40, 41

Operations, 82

Pedagogy, 87
Perry, J., 19, 24, 25
Pintrich, P., 59, 67, 79
Prescriptive rules, 107
Procedural knowledge, 99, 104
Process writing, 18

Reading, 8–11, 14, 19, 20, 36, 38, 39, 41, 121, 126
Register, 106, 109, 110
Rhetoric, 18, 19, 22

Schemata, 70, 80, 81, 86
Schema theory, 79
Situated cognition, 67, 70
Situation theory, 25, 31, 34, 68, 69, 82, 105, 138
Social motives, 21, 22
Strategic approach, 16, 18, 22, 23
Street, B., 6
Studying, 13–15, 23, 28, 36, 38, 39, 40, 60–62, 65, 66, 133
Study skills, 23
Study strategies, 19, 40, 66, 74, 115, 117
Surface approach, 15, 59
Swales, J., 20, 33

Test items, 38
Tests, 61, 62, 65
Textbook, 117, 118, 124, 128, 132, 133

Underachievement, 50

Wittgenstein, L., 8, 74, 120, 121, 175
Writing, 5, 8, 9, 36, 38, 72, 73, 76, 87, 88, 93, 95, 96, 104, 106–112

Xerox Principle, 26

ABOUT THE AUTHOR

Michael Newman is Assistant Professor, Department of Linguistics and Communication Disorders, Queens College/CUNY.